What's on your Mind?

Discover the Power of Biblical Thinking

John Goetsch

Striving Together Publications
4020 E. Lancaster Blvd.
Lancaster, CA 93535
800.201.7748

Edited by Cary Schmidt
Cover design by Andrew Jones
Layout by Craig Parker
Special thanks to our proofreaders.

ISBN 978-1-59894-066-4

Printed in the United States of America

3 Enemies:
World
flesh
devil

HS conviction uses the Word to bring us to repentance.

Warren Wiersbe

The Strategies of Satan

"...for we are not ignorant of his devices." - 2 Corinthians 2:11

Person / Text	Satan's Target	Satan's Weapon	Satan's Purpose	Our Defense
Eve - Gen. 3:1-7 Adam	Eve's mind 2 Cor. 11:3 He wimages it to idol	Lies - John 8:44 Questions God's Word Denies the Word of God Substitute his own lie		God's Word Matt. 4:1-11 We have to know it! Think on it, study it, etc.
Job - Job 1+2 James 5:11	Sin - family, wealth, health	Job's body	Attacks personally + takes all but Job's life.	Impatient w/ God's will
David - 1 Chron. 21 2 Sam. 24	David's will Rom. 12:1-2	Pride James 4:6-7 1 John 2:15-17		Our body is God's; temple - 1 Cor. 6:19 tool - serve God treasury - 2 Cor. 4:7 Imparted grace of God Phil. 1:2-3
Joshua - rep. of the people Zech. 3:1-5 (+ post-exilic book)	Heart + Conscience	Accusers of our heart + mind - no hope, quiet. 2 Cor. 3:6-7,9-11	Indictment by God's will - trying to bring remorse+regret + live in guilt.	Interceding Son of God 1 John 2:1 Christ is our advocate
Ezra, Neh. + Esther are the three post-exile books			Remorse w/o repentance	

2 Cor. 12:7-9

Lord's Day, March 14, 2010

Giving and Attendance:

March 7, 2010

Tithes & Offerings	$5,827.75
Weekly Need	$4,576.92
Sunday School	102
Morning Service	148
Evening Service	59
Wednesday Groups	159

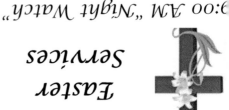

Easter Services

9:00 AM "Night Watch"
(an Easter drama)

Full Breakfast

10:45 AM Easter Service

6:00 PM Communion

Important Summer Dates!!

Warrior Golf Classic - June 5th

VBS - June 13th - 18th

Primaries at Camp Assurance
July 8th-10th

Teens at Camp Joy **July 11-17**

Juniors at Camp Assurance
July 12-16

Nine of our Faith Force enjoyed a great retreat at Camp Joy this weekend, in spite of the weather! Thanks for praying!

Upcoming Events

Mar. 23 Golf Committee Meeting 7 PM

Mar. 26 Men for Christ Conference in Ankeny, Iowa (through Mar. 27)

Mar. 26 FBCS Spring Break through April 5th.

Mar. 29 PrimeTimers dinner & program at Grace Baptist w/ the Mellons, missionaries to Japan. Cost is only $5.00. Sign up in the lobby.

Mar. 30 Deacons' Meeting at 7:00 PM

Apr. 4 Easter Sunday

Apr. 9 Spring Ladies' Retreat at Camp Joy.

Apr. 10 Volleython for Teens

Apr. 11 Benefit Lunch for Eric Albers Illini Central High, Mason City

Apr. 17 Attorney Matt Davis here.

Apr. 24 "Walk for Life" for Esther House

Apr. 25 Evangelistic Meetings with Dave Jaspers (through Wednesday)

May 1 Work Day at Camp Assurance for our men. (Leave April 30th)

May 15 Mother & Daughter Luncheon

Praise the Lord for the excellent work done yesterday morning on the window project. **Phase #1 is now complete!** *Thank you very much* to our talented work crew!

Faith Baptist Church

Schedule for Today:

9:30 AM - Sunday School
Adult Options
Knowing God - Fireside Room
Knowing God's Word - Aud.
Family Life - Room 104

10:45 AM - Morning Worship
Pride and Destruction

4:45 PM - Choir Practice

5:30 PM - Men's Prayer Time
(Room 104 in the basement)

6:00 PM - Evening Service
The Strategies of Satan
(Chart on bulletin back)

S.N.A.C. for Teens

Faith Baptist Church

1501 Howard Court
Pekin, Illinois 61554

Pastoral Staff:
Rev. Timothy Collard, Pastor
Mr. Ken Seest, Assistant Pastor
and FBCS Administrator

Contact us:
309-347-6178
church.secretary@
faithbaptistofpekin.org

This Week at Faith:

Monday: 5:30 PM Sr. Adult Outing at East Peoria China Buffet. (Van leaves from FBC at 4:45 PM.).

Wednesday: 6:45 PM Truth Trackers
6:45 PM Youth Group
7:00 PM Bible Study & Prayer
The Danger of Delay

Wednesday: 8:15 PM FBCS Board Meeting in the fireside room.

Saturday: 8:00 AM *Just Guys* Bible Study in the fireside room. Enjoy spudnuts & coffee at 7:30! Romans 8 is our study topic.

You are invited!
Benefit luncheon for
Eric & Liz Albers
Sunday, April 11, 2010
in *Mason City* at
Illini Central High School
11:30 AM - 5:00 PM
Meal by donation
(Full details on bulletin board)

It's time to register for Camp! See dates at right and get your registrations & deposits turned in to the office. Camp Assurance forms are in the foyer rack; Briar or Karla Trueblood have the forms for Camp Joy.

REFRESH YOUR SOUL

TIMES OF REFRESHING COME FROM THE LORD!

FAITH BAPTIST CHURCH
Pekin, Illinois

TABLE OF CONTENTS

ACKNOWLEDGEMENTS

No doubt you have heard the phrase: "The mind is a terrible thing to waste." Our culture loves being amused but does very little musing. By nature we are lazy mentally and desire that someone else does the thinking for us. Our entertainment certainly bears witness to that fact.

I am grateful for my parents who always challenged me to do my best in school, and for my older sister who set the academic bar high in our family by always bringing home report cards with straight As! While athletics took precedence over academics through my high school years, I will be forever indebted to Coach David Wykes who dared me to get an A from him in my first year of college Greek. He was the first teacher to ever get in my face and motivate me to study.

In my early days of ministry I am thankful for Pastor Clarke Poorman who, as my pastor, took time every day to memorize Scripture with me. Little did he know then how those seeds that he planted in my mind would grow later into such a powerful tool in my life and ministry. I am grateful for my wife and children who never complained about the time that I spent reading, studying, and memorizing.

Since 1996, I have enjoyed being surrounded by a staff at Lancaster Baptist Church and a faculty at West Coast Baptist College who have motivated me to stay sharp in my thinking. And how could I ever thank the hundreds of students who have sat in my classes and asked the tough questions that keep my knees to the floor, my eyes to the skies, and my mind in the Book.

It is my prayer that as you read the pages of this book you will be challenged and changed by *"Casting down imaginations, and every high thing that exalteth itself against the knowledge of God, and bringing into captivity every thought to the obedience of Christ"* (2 Corinthians 10:5).

INTRODUCTION

An empty stomach won't rest until you put something into it. Too bad that isn't true of an empty head! "What were you thinking?" is a question often asked after some unfortunate mistake or blunder. Or, as many a parent has asked their child, "*Why* didn't you think?" Someone has said, "Some people get lost in thought because it's such unfamiliar territory!"

All of us have had times when we have "drawn a blank" or had a "senior moment," but most of us probably wish we could get rid of some thoughts. By no means are we alone in this struggle. Listen to the Apostle Paul as he transparently describes his personal struggle:

> *"For we know that the law is spiritual: but I am carnal, sold under sin. For that which I do I allow not: for what I would, that do I not; but what I hate, that do I. If then I do that which I would not, I consent unto the law that*

it is good. Now then it is no more I that do it, but sin that dwelleth in me. For I know that in me (that is, in my flesh,) dwelleth no good thing: for to will is present with me; but how to perform that which is good I find not. For the good that I would I do not: but the evil which I would not, that I do. Now if I do that I would not, it is no more I that do it, but sin that dwelleth in me. I find then a law, that, when I would do good, evil is present with me. For I delight in the law of God after the inward man: But I see another law in my members, warring against the law of my mind, and bringing me into captivity to the law of sin which is in my members. O wretched man that I am! who shall deliver me from the body of this death? I thank God through Jesus Christ our Lord. So then with the mind I myself serve the law of God; but with the flesh the law of sin."
—ROMANS 7:14–25

Dr. Duane Gish has stated, "The human brain is the most complex arrangement of matter in the universe." Psychologists tell us the average person has about ten thousand thoughts each day. In fact, we are told that regardless of IQ, the average person has more information stored in his brain than is contained in the National Library! The human thought processes remain a mystery to scientists and psychologists. But one thing is sure: How you think will affect the direction of your life. Someone once said, "The body manifests what the mind harbors." American writer and poet, Thomas Bailey Aldrich said, "A man is known by the company his mind keeps."

If we are truly honest, we would admit there are some things we don't like about ourselves—some things we would like to change. Perhaps we recognize that we are prone to be selfish, proud, or covetous. Others may feel they worry too much. Men often admit that they have a problem with their thoughts, while women may concede they hold some bitterness inside. Teenagers might recognize an attitude of anger or rebellion, while older folks may tend to be critical or judgmental. No doubt, we all have our "besetting sin" that seems to be a target for Satan's fiery dart. But what can we do about it? We often hide behind some deadly euphemism, saying, "It's just the way I am" or "my dad was the same way" or "I'm too old to change now."

The truth is, our behavior will change when our thinking changes. If you are stuck in a certain behavioral pattern, you should question your thinking. The Book of Wisdom puts it plainly, *"For as he thinketh in his heart, so is he..."* (Proverbs 23:7). We must watch our thoughts for they are blueprints for our actions. A thought that dominates you inwardly will ultimately drive you outwardly. Certain thought

The average person has 10,000 thoughts every day.

patterns are often deeply engrained, but it is never impossible through the power of God to change them. The members of the church at Corinth were saved out of some pretty wicked lifestyles (See 1 Corinthians 6:9–11), and their minds had been tainted by sin which was now affecting their behavior as believers. Paul reminds them that change is possible, but only as they would allow the power of God to change their thinking. *"For though we walk in the flesh, we do not war after the flesh: (For the weapons of our warfare are not carnal, but mighty through God to the pulling down of strong holds;) Casting down imaginations and every high thing that exalteth itself against the knowledge of God, and bringing into captivity every thought to the obedience of Christ"* (2 Corinthians 10:3–5).

With ten thousand thoughts whirling through our brains daily, we're going to need more than human will power to keep them all pure and God-honoring. We need to let the mind of the Master be the master of our minds. Change must always take place from the inside out. Listen to what Paul reminds the Ephesians about this work of the Spirit of God in the inner man:

> *"That he would grant you, according to the riches of his glory, to be strengthened with might by his Spirit in the inner man; That Christ may dwell in your hearts by faith; that ye, being rooted and grounded in love, May be able to comprehend with all saints what is the breadth, and length, and depth, and height; And to know the love of Christ, which passeth knowledge, that ye might be filled with all the fullness of God. Now unto him that is able to do exceeding abundantly above all that we ask or think, according to the power that worketh in us."*
> —EPHESIANS 3:16–20

I know what you're saying—everywhere we go and everything we see in our present culture is stimulating us to think the wrong thoughts. We'll talk more about this stimuli later in this book, but for now claim the promise of God's Word:

> *"Be careful for nothing; but in every thing by prayer and supplication with thanksgiving let your requests be made known unto God. And the peace of God, which passeth all understanding, shall keep your hearts **and minds** through Christ Jesus. Finally, brethren, whatsoever things are true, whatsoever things are honest, whatsoever things are just, whatsoever things are pure, whatsoever things are lovely, whatsoever things are of good report; if there be any virtue, and if there be any praise **think on these things**. Those things, which ye have both learned, and received, and heard, and seen in me, do: and the God of peace shall be with you."* [Emphasis mine]
> —PHILIPPIANS 4:6–9

Are you willing to let God control your thoughts? If He doesn't, something else will. Too many of us sit back in life and let our environment influence our thoughts. The Turks have an old proverb that reads, "The devil tempts all other men, but the idle man tempts the devil." In a sermon entitled "The Guide to the Mind," Robert AuBuchon Jr. gives an illustration entitled "The Stranger."

A few months before I was born, my Dad met a stranger who was new to our small Tennessee town. From the beginning, Dad was fascinated with this enchanting newcomer, and soon invited him to live with our family.

The stranger was quickly accepted and was around to welcome me into the world a few months later. As I grew up I never questioned his place in our family. In my young mind, each member had a special niche. My brother, Bill, five years my senior, was my example. Fran, my younger sister, gave me an opportunity to play 'big brother' and develop the art of teasing.

My parents were complementary instructors— Mom taught me to love the Word of God, and Dad taught me to obey it. But the stranger was our storyteller. He could weave the most fascinating tales. Adventures, mysteries and comedies were daily conversations. He could hold our whole family spell-bound for hours each evening.

If I wanted to know about politics, history, or science, he knew it all. He knew about the past, understood the present, and seemingly could predict the future. The pictures he could draw were so life like that I would often laugh or cry as I watched. He was like a friend to the whole family. He took Dad, Bill and me to our first major league baseball game. He was always encouraging us to see the movies and he even made arrangements to introduce us to several movie stars. My brother and I were deeply impressed by John Wayne in particular.

The stranger was an incessant talker. Dad didn't seem to mind, but sometimes Mom would quietly get up—while the rest of us were enthralled with one of his stories of faraway places—go to her room, read her Bible and pray. I wonder now if she ever prayed that the stranger would leave.

You see, my Dad ruled our household with certain moral convictions, but this stranger never felt obligated to honor them. Profanity, for example, was not allowed in our house—not from us, our friends, or adults. Our longtime visitor, however, used occasional four letter words that burned my ears and made Dad squirm. To my knowledge the stranger was never confronted.

My Dad was a teetotaler who didn't permit alcohol in his home—not even for cooking. But the stranger felt like we needed exposure and enlightened us to other ways of life. He offered us beer and other alcoholic beverages often. He made cigarettes look tasty, cigars manly, and pipes distinguished. He talked freely (probably too freely) about sex. His comments were sometimes blatant, sometimes suggestive, and generally embarrassing. I know now that my early concepts of the man-woman relationship were influenced by the stranger.

As I look back, I believe it was the grace of God that the stranger did not influence us more. Time after time he opposed the values of my parents. Yet he was seldom rebuked and never asked to leave.

More than thirty years have passed since the stranger moved in with the young family on Morningside Drive. He is not nearly so intriguing to my Dad as he was in those early years. But if I were to walk into my parents' den today, you would still see him sitting over in a corner, waiting for someone to listen to him talk and watch him draw his pictures.

His name? We called him TV (Robert AuBuchon, RFTPsermons.com, *The Guide to the Mind*).

So, what's on your mind? If the thoughts of your heart became a reality in your actions, what kind of a person would you be? God's Word tells us that we are headed in the direction of our thoughts. Your desires will become your destination. God's will for every Christian is that we be Christ-like so the lost and dying world around us can see God in us.

> *"But ye are a chosen generation, a royal priesthood, an holy nation, a peculiar people; that ye should shew forth the praises of him who called you out of darkness into his marvellous light: Which in time past were not a people, but are now the people of God: which had not obtained mercy, but now have obtained mercy. Dearly beloved, I beseech you as strangers and pilgrims, abstain from fleshly lusts, which war against the soul; Having your conversation honest among the Gentiles: that, whereas they speak against you as evildoers, they may by your good works, which they shall behold, glorify God in the day of visitation."*—1 PETER 2:9–12

If the unsaved person could see what's on your mind right now, would they be led toward Christ? That's a pretty scary thought, isn't it? But the truth is, whatever is on your mind will soon become your manner, and while the world can't read your mind, they can read your manners. *"Ye are our epistle written in our hearts, known and read of all men: Forasmuch as ye are manifestly declared to be the epistle of Christ ministered by us, written not with ink, but with the Spirit of the living God; not in tables of stone, but in fleshy tables of the heart"* (2 Corinthians 3:2–3).

We are headed in the direction of our thoughts.

God desires that our entire lives be wholly surrendered to His control. We can't do that on our own, but there is a first step that we all must take. *"I beseech you therefore, brethren, by the mercies* *of God, that ye present your bodies a living sacrifice, holy, acceptable unto God, which is your reasonable service. And be not conformed to this world: but be ye transformed **by the renewing of your mind**, that ye may prove what is that good, and acceptable, and perfect, will of God"* [Emphasis mine] (Romans 12:1–2). Erwin W. Lutzer states, "The difference between worldliness and godliness is a renewed mind" (Erwin W. Lutzer, *Winning the Inner War*, Colorado Springs, CO, Victor—Cook Communications Ministries, 1979, p. 71).

So, are you ready to change your mind? Let's get started.

1

PART ONE

Brainwashed Christianity

Has anyone ever said to you, "A penny for your thoughts?" There are times in life when it would be interesting to be a mind-reader. God, however, never has to wonder what's on your mind; He already knows. I'm sure Noah and his family were aware of how wicked their culture had become. Just a few generations after the fall, society had sunk to the depths of depravity. Looking past the outer manifestations of sin, God's laser-like eyes could see right to the source of the problem. *"And God saw that the wickedness of man was great in the earth,* **and that every imagination of the thoughts of his heart** *was only evil continually"* [Emphasis mine] (Genesis 6:5). The actions of man were merely a result of his thoughts.

David understood that God knows our thoughts. He gives good counsel to his son, *"And thou, Solomon my son, know thou the God of thy father, and serve him with a perfect heart and a* **willing mind:** *for the LORD searcheth all hearts, and* **understandeth all the**

imaginations of the thoughts" [Emphasis mine] (1 Chronicles 28:9).
We think we can conceal our thoughts and we get pretty good at
masking them, but the prophet of old cut right through the façade,
"...for I know the things that come into your mind, every one of them"
(Ezekiel 11:5). We have never had a thought, a desire, a motive, an
attitude, a whim, or a dream that God didn't clearly know!

As normal human beings, we enjoy things that are clean—clean
hands, clean silverware, clean clothes and a clean car. We build our
houses with sinks and showers. We install dishwashers and washing
machines. Frequent trips to the car wash are essential to taking care
of our vehicles. You feel better after a shower and enjoy putting on
some clean clothes. No one wants to eat with a dirty fork or drive
a car that's filthy. So why do we put up with a polluted mind? Why
do we go day after day, week after week, year after year with layers
of filth covering our minds? Do you need to be brainwashed?

We hear a lot about water pollution, air pollution, noise
pollution, and sight pollution. We're worried about the ozone layer
of the earth's atmosphere being destroyed because of all the harmful
chemicals that are coming from our houses and automobiles. But
it's time we get concerned about mind pollution! Long before there
were environmentalists and ecologists demanding to be heard,

What can wash away my sin? Nothing but the blood of Jesus;
What can make me whole again? Nothing but the blood of Jesus.
For my pardon this I see—Nothing but the blood of Jesus;
For my cleansing, this my plea—Nothing but the blood of Jesus.
Nothing can for sin atone—Nothing but the blood of Jesus;
Naught of good that I have done—Nothing but the blood of Jesus.
This is all my hope and peace—Nothing but the blood of Jesus;
This is all my righteousness—Nothing but the blood of Jesus.
Oh precious is the flow that makes me white as snow;
No other fount I know, Nothing but the blood of Jesus.
—ROBERT LOWRY

Micah the prophet was sounding an alarm, *"Arise ye, and depart; for this is not your rest: because it is polluted, it shall destroy you, even with a sore destruction"* (Micah 2:10). Indeed, filthy brains lead to faulty behavior. If we don't get to the brainwash today, we will wake up from a behavior-wreck tomorrow.

This cleansing that is so needed today starts with salvation. Try as we may through our own efforts, we can never cleanse ourselves from our sin nature. *"But we are all as an unclean thing, and all our righteousnesses are as filthy rags; and we all do fade as a leaf; and our iniquities, like the wind, have taken us away"* (Isaiah 64:6). A thousand moral deeds and a million religious rituals can never wash away the sin on our hearts. Initial cleansing from sin can only come through the Person who declares, *"Come now, and let us reason together, saith the LORD: though your sins be as scarlet, they shall be as white as snow; though they be red like crimson, they shall be as wool"* (Isaiah 1:18). The blood of Jesus Christ that was shed on Calvary's cross is the only cleansing agent for sin. *"How much more shall the blood of Christ, who through the eternal Spirit offered himself without spot to God, purge your conscience from dead works to serve the living God?"* (Hebrews 9:14). The Christians at Corinth knew all about the truth of William Cowper's hymn long before it was penned: "There is a fountain filled with blood; Drawn from Immanuel's veins; And sinners, plunged beneath that flood, Lose all their guilty stains."

*"Know ye not that the unrighteous shall not inherit the kingdom of God? Be not deceived: neither fornicators, nor idolaters, nor adulterers, nor effeminate, nor abusers of themselves with mankind, Nor thieves, nor covetous, nor drunkards, nor revilers, nor extortioners, shall inherit the kingdom of God. And such were some of you: but **ye are washed**, but ye are sanctified, but ye are justified in the name of the Lord Jesus, and by the Spirit of our God"* [Emphasis mine] (1 Corinthians 6:9–11). If you have never experienced the joy of having your sins forgiven, call upon Christ today. His blood has

the power to cleanse you of your sinful past and give you eternal life in Heaven.

As children of God, we are not exempt from allowing the filth of sin to stain our lives. *Positionally*, we have been cleansed by the blood of Christ and are before God justified from our sin. But *practically*, we still battle on a daily basis the pollutions of this old world. King David had succumbed to the temptation of sin. Lustful thoughts led to adultery, deception, and even murder! This is a sad state of affairs for a "man after God's own heart." David knew where to go for cleansing. He cries from the depth of his soul, *"Have mercy upon me, O God, according to thy lovingkindness: according unto the multitude of thy tender mercies blot out my transgressions. Wash me throughly from mine iniquity, and cleanse me from my sin"* (Psalm 51:1–2).

Is it time for a brainwash? Is God inviting you to cleanse your mind as He did the city of Jerusalem? *"O Jerusalem, wash thine heart from wickedness, that thou mayest be saved. How long shall thy vain thoughts lodge within thee?"* (Jeremiah 4:14). How much longer will you go with your mind filled with empty and wicked thoughts? Remember, if God isn't in control of your mind, you will soon lose control of your manners.

In the latter half of Acts 17, we find the Apostle Paul making his way to a place called Mars' Hill. As he arrives, he observes these intellectual people steeped in pagan pluralism. They had altars for every kind of god you could think of. They had even erected one "TO THE UNKNOWN GOD." It appears that their intellectualism had caused them to stop thinking. It reminds me of the dad who bought a bicycle for his son. After opening the box and looking at the large booklet of instructions on how to assemble the bike, he was totally confused. For the life of him, he couldn't follow the step-by-step instructions outlined in the manual. Finally, he sought the help of an old handyman who lived next door. The old fellow picked up the pieces, studied them, and then began assembling the bicycle. In a short time, he had it put together. "That's amazing," said the dad, "and you did it without even looking at the instructions!" "Fact is," said the old man, "I can't read, and when a fellow can't read, he's got to think."

A lot of people today are *"professing themselves to be wise,"* and they have become *"fools"* (Romans 1:22). Paul challenges these intellectuals on Mars' Hill to start thinking correctly. The brainwashed person will come to **Four Realizations...**

CHAPTER ONE

The Realization of a Created Mind

No computer can or ever will match the ability of the human brain. Our minds have an amazing capacity to receive, store, and process information at unbelievable speeds and in unparalleled amounts.

Our Minds Are Designed Creations

The Architect and Creator of all things is God Himself. *"All things were made by him; and without him was not any thing made that was made"* (John 1:3). The "self-made" man does not exist! *"A man can receive nothing, except it be given him from heaven"* (John 3:27). Man boasts of his knowledge and skill, but without God, we can do nothing. *"For who maketh thee to differ from another? and what hast thou that thou didst not receive? now if thou didst receive it, why dost thou glory, as if thou hadst not received it?"* (1 Corinthians 4:7).

To be honest, I don't think that I have enough faith to be an evolutionist. To believe that we evolved over billions of years from a tiny amoeba that was floating in water (of course we have not yet explained where the water came from, or the planet on which the water existed), takes a lot of faith. There are just too many gaps in that theory that must be filled with enormous faith for me to believe it.

Of all creation, only man can say yes or no to God.

I find it a lot easier to believe by faith the words of the psalmist, *"By the word of the LORD were the heavens made; and all the host of them by the breath of his mouth. He gathereth the waters of the sea together as an heap: he layeth up the depth in storehouses. Let all the earth fear the LORD: let all the inhabitants of the world stand in awe of him. For he spake, and it was done; he commanded, and it stood fast"* (Psalm 33:6–9).

And perhaps the most intricate of all creations is the human body.

> *"For thou hast possessed my reins; thou hast covered me in my mother's womb. I will praise thee; for I am fearfully and wonderfully made: marvellous are thy works; and that my soul knoweth right well. My substance was not hid from thee, when I was made in secret, and curiously wrought in the lowest parts of the earth. Thine eyes did see my substance, yet being unperfect; and in thy book all my members were written, which in continuance were fashioned, when as yet there was none of them. How precious also are thy thoughts unto me, O God! how great is the sum of them."*—PSALM 139:13–17

Paul begins his address to those on Mars' Hill by saying, *"God that made the world and all things therein, seeing that he is Lord of heaven and earth, dwelleth not in temples made with hands; Neither is worshipped with men's hands, as though he needed any thing, seeing he giveth to all life, and breath, and all things"* (Acts 17:24–25). Our bodies and minds are **Designed Creations**.

Our Minds Are under a Divine Control.

As part of God's creation, <u>we are not in charge!</u> The minds that God has created within us have astounding capabilities, but they are limited. Only God is omniscient. We are limited in our knowledge because God has placed a boundary on our minds. *"The secret things belong unto the Lord our God: but those things which are revealed belong unto us and to our children for ever, that we may do all the words of this law"* (Deuteronomy 29:29). While man has accumulated information for centuries so that we as individuals do not have to learn everything from scratch, God still declares, *"For my thoughts are not your thoughts, neither are your ways my ways, saith the Lord. For as the heavens are higher than the earth, so are my ways higher than your ways, and my thoughts than your thoughts"* (Isaiah 55:8–9).

Paul reminds these intellectuals that God *"hath made of one blood all nations of men for to dwell on the face of the earth, and hath determined the times before appointed, and the **bounds of their habitation"*** [Emphasis mine] (Acts 17:26). When I hear of the development of science in areas like cloning, I wonder if we are getting close to the boundary that God has set for our minds. There are many things that God knows are best that we do not know. Don't let what you can't understand weaken your faith. I can't humanly explain the eternal being of God. I can't put into human terms the fact that God had no beginning but has always existed. That is impossible for me to fathom, but my inability to explain it makes it no less true. That's where faith enters the equation.

And one day our faith will become sight! *"For now we see through a glass, darkly; but then face to face: now I know in part; but then shall I know even as also I am known"* (1 Corinthians 13:12). Our good God has placed **A Divine Control** upon our minds.

Our Minds Can Make Deliberate Choices

Along with the ability of our minds to receive, process, and store information, God has given us the ability to make choices about that information. Paul reminds the audience that they have a choice about whom they will worship. *"That they should seek the Lord, if haply they might feel after him, and find him, though he be not far from every one of us. For in him we live, and move, and have our being; as certain also of your own poets have said, For we are also his offspring"* (Acts 17:27–28).

Animals are created with an instinctive reflex—they don't think before they react. If you surprisingly pull a dog's ears, he may bite you (the book of Proverbs tells you that is a very unwise thing to do) because he is simply reacting to an adverse stimuli. The human brain however has the ability to pause between stimuli and response so that a right choice can be made.

God has created a "buffer" between the stimulus and the response. Scientists have been studying the brain for years and while there is much to learn, here is what they say about the human mind's capability of choice: "Neuronal activity begins in the sensory areas of the brain for as much as a second before voluntary motor activity occurs. Also, neuronal activity begins in the premotor areas of the cortex and in some areas of the basal ganglia many milliseconds before motor activity occurs in the motor cortex. Therefore, it is currently thought that cerebration occurring in these integrative portions of the brain, operating in association with the cerebellum, conceives and plans the complex sequence of movements that is to be executed. Only after the plan has been established is the primary motor system set into action to cause the sequential movements" (Arthur C. Guyton, *Human Physiology and Mechanisms of Disease*, Philadelphia, W.B. Saunders Company, 1987, p. 413).

This is why we come to understand that to be tempted is not sin—even Jesus *"was in all points tempted like as we are, yet without sin"* (Hebrews 4:15). In other words, the same wrong stimuli that calls to us every day likewise tempted our Saviour. But in that moment of choice, He did not sin—for He was God. In that split second of time, between temptation and response, our minds have the ability to choose. Think about the following two stories from Scripture. In both cases there was temptation, but the choices made were very different.

> *"Now the serpent was more subtil than any beast of the field which the LORD God had made. And he said unto the woman, Yea, hath God said, Ye shall not eat of every tree of the garden? And the woman said unto the serpent, We may eat of the fruit of the trees of the garden: But of the fruit of the tree which is in the midst of the garden, God hath said, Ye shall not eat of it, neither shall ye touch it, lest ye die. And the serpent said unto the woman, Ye shall not surely die: For God doth know that in the day ye eat thereof, then your eyes shall be opened, and ye shall be as gods, knowing good and evil. And when the woman saw that the tree was good for food, and that it was pleasant to the eyes, and a tree to be desired to make one wise, she took of the fruit thereof, and did eat, and gave also unto her husband with her; and he did eat."*—GENESIS 3:1–6

Only two choices on the shelf: pleasing God or pleasing self.
—Ken Collier

> *"And it came to pass after these things, that his master's wife cast her eyes upon Joseph; and she said, Lie with me. But he refused, and said unto his master's wife, Behold, my master wotteth not what is with me in the house, and he hath committed all that he hath to my hand; There is none greater in this house than*

I; neither hath he kept back any thing from me but thee, because thou art his wife: how then can I do this great wickedness, and sin against God? And it came to pass, as she spake to Joseph day by day, that he hearkened not unto her, to lie by her, or to be with her."—GENESIS 39:7–10

What a difference a simple choice made in these lives. Both were tempted—that wasn't the sin—it was what they did with that temptation that made the difference between right and wrong. We are not simply "products of our environment" as Sigmund Freud and Carl Rogers would have us believe, nor are we simply conditioned in our behavior by stimuli as B.F. Skinner and others would teach. We are products of our choices conceived in our minds and carried out in our actions. No one can make us do wrong without our consent. Solomon of old understood well the power of choices and advised his son, *"…if sinners entice thee, consent thou not"* (Proverbs 1:10).

The human mind—what a fascinating work of God! A **Designed Creation** under **Divine Control** with an ability to make **Deliberate Choices.** It would be wise for us to daily ask our Creator to *"Let the words of my mouth, and the meditation of my heart, be acceptable in thy sight, O LORD, my strength and my redeemer"* (Psalm 19:14).

Study Questions

1. Who is the creator of your mind? See John 1:3.

2. What is the most intricate of all creations? See Psalm 139:13–17.

3. In a split second of time between temptation and response, our mind has the ability to make a choice. Compare and contrast the following stories in the Bible: Eve and the serpent (Genesis 3:1–6) and Joseph (Genesis 39:7–10). How were their responses to temptation different? Were their temptations similar?

4. God has placed boundaries on your mind—your knowledge and understanding. Do you find yourself trusting your logic—your limited mind—instead of God's omniscience? List five areas in your life in which you need to trust God.

5. Write out the wise counsel David gave to his son in 1 Chronicles 28:9.

Memory Verse

"For my thoughts are not your thoughts, neither are your ways my ways, saith the LORD. For as the heavens are higher than the earth, so are my ways higher than your ways, and my thoughts than your thoughts."—ISAIAH 55:8–9

CHAPTER TWO

The Realization of a Changed Mind

P aul now begins to challenge the thinking of those who were gathered there on Mars' Hill. While they were very open-minded to the pluralistic thinking of their day, Paul admonishes them to "change their minds." *"Forasmuch then as we are the offspring of God, we **ought not to think** that the Godhead is like unto gold, or silver, or stone, graven by art and man's device. And the times of this ignorance God winked at; but now commandeth all men everywhere to repent"* [Emphasis mine] (Acts 17:29–30). Their thinking about God was wrong and needed to be changed. That wrong thinking is a result of the sin nature.

Not only are we born sinners, we are born with a sin nature. That is, our very being or make-up is sinful. Thus, not only do we do wrong things naturally, we think wrong things naturally. *"And you hath he quickened, who were dead in trespasses and sins; Wherein in time past ye walked according to the course of this world, according to the prince of the power of the air, the spirit that now worketh* *in the children of disobedience: Among whom also we all had our conversation in times past in the lusts of our flesh, fulfilling the desires of the flesh **and of the mind**; and were by nature the children of wrath, even as others"* [Emphasis mine] (Ephesians 2:1–3). A man in his natural sinful state does sinful things, but he also thinks sinfully, because his mind is sinful. *"Unto the pure all things are pure: but unto them that are defiled and unbelieving is nothing pure; **but even their mind and conscience is defiled**"* [Emphasis mine] (Titus 1:15). We often focus on the lifestyle that needs to change at salvation, but conversion also involves a changed mind. (Interestingly, the word *repentance* simply means "a change of mind.")

Now it is natural to think we are doing okay until we meet someone doing better. Never is this more evident than when we come face to face with God! *"In the year that king Uzziah died I saw also the Lord sitting upon a throne, high and lifted up, and his train filled the temple.... Then said I, Woe is me! for I am undone; because I am a man of unclean lips, and I dwell in the midst of a people of unclean lips: for mine eyes have seen the King, the LORD of hosts"* (Isaiah 6:1, 5). *"If I had not come and spoken unto them, they had not had sin: but now they have no cloak for their sin"* (John 15:22). Paul pulls the cloak from off their wrong thinking by presenting the "unknown" God to them.

I serve a risen Savior, He's in the world today;
I know that He is living, whatever men may say;
I see His hand of mercy, I hear His voice of cheer,
And just the time I need Him He's always near.
He lives, He lives, Christ Jesus lives today!
He walks with me and talks with me along life's narrow way.
He lives, He lives, salvation to impart!
You ask me how I know He lives? He lives within my heart.
—ALFRED H. ACKLEY

He Presents a Living God

"Forasmuch then as we are the offspring of God, we ought not to think that the Godhead is like unto gold, or silver, or stone, graven by art and man's device" (Acts 17:29). While the altars on Mars' Hill were beautifully carved and adorned, they all had one thing in common. They were all lifeless! Paul says, "You've been thinking all wrong. Let me introduce you to Someone who is alive!" Jeremiah says, *"But the LORD is the true God, he is the living God, and an everlasting king"* (Jeremiah 10:10). The gods of this world offer no hope, for they have no life. Man is looking for peace, joy, fulfillment, and contentment, but it will never be found in stone statues or golden figurines. The sinful nature leaves man's soul parched and dry and as the psalmist he cries, *"My soul thirsteth for God, for **the living God**"* [Emphasis mine] (Psalm 42:2). On a gloomy day in Bethany, Jesus stood in a graveyard. All around him the sobbing of those grieving could be heard, for the sting of death had been felt once again. But the imps of Hell trembled when He, the Son of God, lifted His voice above the cloud of despair and cried, *"I am the resurrection, and the life: he that believeth in me, though he were dead, yet shall he live: And whosoever liveth and believeth in me shall never die"* (John 11:25–26).

King Darius changed his mind about **the living God**. Regrettably, the king had allowed his entourage to trick him into signing a decree that was sure to send Daniel to a den of lions. The writing was signed and could not be changed *"according to the law of the Medes and the Persians, which altereth not"* (Daniel 6:8). The king knew he had made a mistake, yet he had no choice but to put Daniel into that lions' den. But that's not the end of the story!

> *"And a stone was brought, and laid upon the mouth of the den; and the king sealed it with his own signet, and with the signet of his lords; that the purpose might not be changed concerning Daniel. Then the king went to*

his palace, and passed the night fasting: neither were instruments of musick brought before him: and his sleep went from him. Then the king arose very early in the morning, and went in haste unto the den of lions. And when he came to the den, he cried with a lamentable voice unto Daniel: and the king spake and said to Daniel, O Daniel, servant of **the living God***, is thy God, whom thou servest continually, able to deliver thee from the den of lions? Then said Daniel unto the king, O king, live for ever. My God hath sent his angel, and hath shut the lions' mouths, that they have not hurt me....And the king commanded, and they brought those men which had accused Daniel, and they cast them into the den of lions, them, their children, and their wives; and the lions had the mastery of them, and brake all their bones in pieces or ever they came at the bottom of the den. Then king Darius wrote unto all people, nations, and languages, that dwell in all the earth; Peace be multiplied unto you. I make a decree, That in every dominion of my kingdom men tremble and fear before the God of Daniel: for he is* **the living God***, and stedfast forever, and his kingdom that which shall not be destroyed, and his dominion shall be even unto the end. He delivereth and rescueth, and he worketh signs and wonders in heaven and in earth, who hath delivered Daniel from the power of the lions."* [Emphasis mine]
—DANIEL 6:17–22, 24–27

What gods are you trusting in to deliver you? Will your idol of money, or power, or sex deliver you from the power of sin and death? It's time to change your mind! We need people today like those in Thessalonica who *"…turned to God from idols to serve **the living and true God**"* [Emphasis mine] (1 Thessalonians 1:9).

He Presents a Longsuffering God

"And the times of this ignorance God winked at" (Acts 17:30). God could have made all of those altars on Mars' Hill fall over. (The god Dagon had a little trouble staying on his feet back in the Old Testament.) But God is a patient, longsuffering God. *"It is of the LORD's mercies that we are not consumed, because his compassions fail not. They are new every morning: great is thy faithfulness"* (Lamentations 3:22–23). Aren't you glad that God is a God of second chances? I have heard it said that the average person hears the Gospel forty times before he gets saved! What a patient God. *"The LORD is merciful and gracious, slow to anger, and plenteous in mercy"* (Psalm 103:8).

God is so unlike us. We are not very quick to give someone a second chance, much less a third, a fourth, or a fortieth! If you and I were God, Heaven would be empty. But, *"The Lord is not slack concerning his promise, as some men count slackness; **but is longsuffering** to us-ward, not willing that any should perish, but that all should come to repentance"* [Emphasis mine] (2 Peter 3:9). In fact, *"Who is a God like unto thee, that pardoneth iniquity, and passeth by the transgression of the remnant of his heritage? he retaineth not his anger for ever, **because he delighteth in mercy**"* [Emphasis mine] (Micah 7:18). The longsuffering of God ought to be enough to change anyone's mind.

Our God is **A Living God** and **A Longsuffering God**, but then…

He Presents a Lawful God

Don't get too comfortable with God's patience. He has winked at this ignorance, *"…but now commandeth all men everywhere to repent"* (Acts 17:30). Notice this is not a suggestion; it is a command! And it's for all men—everywhere! It is not just for the reprobate, but for the religious. It is not just for the one who sits in prison, but for the one who sits in the pews.

Ever since the first sin, man has followed Adam's example of blaming his sin on others, rationalizing it away and finding some kind of man-made fig leaves to cover it up. Sin is not judged by the way *we* see it, but by the way *God* sees it. Sin is not on the judgment stand here; the sinner is! God is not speaking to the *sin* here, but to the *sinner*. The problem is not in the *deed* of sin; it is in the *doer* of the deed. Sin isn't going to change, but we as sinners must. *"Repent therefore of this thy wickedness, and pray God, if perhaps **the thought of thine heart** may be forgiven thee"* [Emphasis mine] (Acts 8:22).

Too often, man changes his actions when he gets caught, but never changes his mind about sin. In fact, to most people today, it's not sin unless you get caught! For sure, it is our actions that remind us that there is a problem of sin and we need to stop. But notice how God's instructions about repentance go beyond the actions, *"…Repent, and turn yourselves from all your transgressions; so iniquity shall not be your ruin. Cast away from you all your transgressions, whereby ye have transgressed; and make you **a new heart** and **a new spirit**: for why will ye die, O house of Israel?"* [Emphasis mine] (Ezekiel 18:30–31).

> *Sin is not judged by the way we see it, but by the way God sees it.*

Nothing will change as long as we compare ourselves with the status quo of humanity around us. We probably stack up pretty well compared to the majority, but to do so is a huge mistake. *"For we dare not make ourselves of the number, or compare ourselves with some that commend themselves: but they measuring themselves by themselves, and comparing themselves among themselves, are not wise"* (2 Corinthians 10:12). We must place ourselves next to **A Living God; A Longsuffering God;** and **A Lawful God.** When we do, we'll quickly see the need for *A Changed Mind.*

Study Questions

1. Write out the words that describe God in Psalm 103:8.

2. What does God command of every man in Acts 17:30?

3. How does the story of Daniel in the lions' den prove the fact that a living God does exist. See Daniel 6:18–27.

4. Ezekiel 18:30 says, "...*Repent, and turn yourselves from all your transgressions; so iniquity shall not be your ruin.*" Write down the sins with which you struggle most. Review this list and repent of your sins to your Heavenly Father. Then, explain how you plan to turn from these transgressions the next time Satan tries to tempt you with them.

5. Write out the command of repentance in Acts 8:22.

Memory Verse

"It is of the LORD's mercies that we are not consumed, because his compassions fail not. They are new every morning: great is thy faithfulness."—LAMENTATIONS 3:22–23

CHAPTER THREE

The Realization of a Conscientious Mind

When a change of mind takes place (repentance), the conscience becomes sensitive again. <u>Sin has a deadening effect on our hearts.</u> Paul speaks about this process that takes place over time, *"Now the Spirit speaketh expressly, that in the latter times some shall depart from the faith, giving heed to seducing spirits, and doctrines of devils; Speaking lies in hypocrisy; having their conscience seared with a hot iron"* (1 Timothy 4:1–2).

Years ago I had the privilege of witnessing to an old rancher in Montana by the name of Holly Croy. He didn't have much time for me as he thought all preachers were lazy and not worth much. Having been raised on a farm, I decided to try to prove to him that I could work as hard as he could. I arrived the next morning at 5:00 AM to help him brand his cattle. What an experience! For the next ten hours I wrestled with steers in the dirt and manure of that outdoor corral. Mr. Croy branded the old-fashioned way—rope the steers, tackle them to the ground, get the hot irons out of the fire, and apply that red-hot metal to the flank. Those cows would bawl and jerk and it took every fiber of my body to hold them down. The stench of the burning flesh stayed in my nostrils for weeks afterwards. (By the way, Holly did come to church that week. Years later, two weeks before he died, his wife had the privilege of leading him to Christ.)

When that hot iron is placed on the flank of an animal, it hurts—big time! But once that flesh is "seared" with the hot iron, it is deadened to all feeling. From that point on that branded area of flesh is crusty and hard. The animal has no feeling in that area. The effects of sin are the same upon our minds. Where we were once sensitive and troubled, we now sense little of the convicting power of God. *"He, that being often reproved hardeneth his neck"* (Proverbs 29:1). *"Who being past feeling have given themselves over unto lasciviousness, to work all uncleanness with greediness"* (Ephesians 4:19).

But there is hope, *"For the word of God is quick, and powerful, and sharper than any twoedged sword, piercing even to the dividing asunder of soul and spirit, and of the joints and marrow, and is a **discerner of the thoughts and intents of the heart"** [Emphasis mine] (Hebrews 4:12). And that is exactly why the apostle stands to preach here in the midst of all the pagan altars. He is fully aware that there is but one thing that can break through the hardness of these hearts and bring about a change of mind. No doubt the words of the weeping prophet burned in his heart as he spoke, *"The prophet that hath a dream, let him tell a dream; and he that hath my word, let him speak my word faithfully. What is the chaff to the wheat? saith the LORD. Is not my word like as a fire? saith the LORD; and like a hammer that breaketh the rock in pieces?"* (Jeremiah 23:28–29).

God's Word Declares an Inescapable Reckoning

"Because he hath appointed a day, in the which he will judge the world in righteousness by that man whom he hath ordained" (Acts 17:31).

When God's Word begins to break through, it sobers us to the fact that we are accountable to God. Daniel Webster was once asked, "What is the greatest thought that can occupy a man's mind?" After a slight hesitation, he responded, "The greatest thought that can occupy a man's mind is his accountability to God."

Dr. Bob Jones, Sr. was working in his office one day at Bob Jones College in Cleveland, Tennessee, when a student walked in unannounced. Dr. Jones, sensing that someone had stepped into the room, said without looking up from his work, "May I help you?" The young lady responded, "I just came to tell you that I am going to kill myself." Without taking his eyes off of his work, Dr. Jones said, "I'm sorry, you can't do that." She said, "I'm not kidding, I'm going to commit suicide!" Dr. Jones again responded with, "I'm sorry, you can't." Raising her voice, the young lady said, "Don't make fun of me! I'm tired of living. I'm going to end it all today!" Looking up into her eyes, Dr. Jones said firmly, "I'm sorry, you can't do that. You're going to live somewhere forever."

Life—our opportunity to prepare to meet God.

How true his statement was, for *"…as it is appointed unto men once to die, but after this the judgment"* (Hebrews 9:27). We may be well prepared for life, but are we prepared to die? Our families, our jobs, our social standing, our finances may all be in good order, but God says, *"Prepare to meet thy God"* (Amos 4:12). When you boil it all down, life is nothing more than our opportunity to prepare to meet God! It is **An Inescapable Reckoning.**

God's Word Declares an Incredible Reality

God's Word always gets personal. We don't mind sermons that condemn David, or Peter, or Judas. Secretly, we hope sinners get what they deserve. But when God's finger points at us—now that's a different story.

The Spirit of God now gazes into the eyes of these religious intellectuals on Mars' Hill as Paul declares, *"…whereof he hath given assurance unto **all men**, in that he hath raised him from the dead"* [Emphasis mine] (Acts 17:31). No one is exempt from this appointment with God. Earthly power will win you no favors. Earthly riches will not bribe you an escape. Your social graces and popularity will be worthless as you stand alone before God! People convince themselves that a loving God would not send anyone to Hell—surely He will allow them past His judgment into Heaven. Listen to the sobering words of Ezekiel, *"Now is the end come upon thee, and I will send mine anger upon thee, and will judge thee according to thy ways, and will recompense upon thee all thine abominations. And mine eye shall not spare thee, neither will I have pity: but I will recompense thy ways upon thee, and thine abominations shall be in the midst of thee: and ye shall know that I am the LORD"* (Ezekiel 7:3–4). Later in the same chapter he informs us that our money will not bribe God, *"They shall cast their silver in the streets, and their gold shall be removed: their silver and their gold shall not be able to deliver them in the day of the wrath of the LORD: they shall not satisfy their souls, neither fill their bowels: because it is the stumblingblock of their iniquity"* (Ezekiel 7:19).

As a kid, I dreaded going to the dentist. (I'm still not really fond of it.) My parents would make me go, and I always had cavities. I inherited soft teeth from my father and no matter how hard I brushed, the dentist chair became my "electric chair" every visit. I can still hear that old rotary drill grinding inside my mouth. Without numbing gel or gas, I can still feel that electric bolt of pain striking the nerve of my jaw and reverberating all the way down to my toes! When I went to college I decided I would never make another dentist appointment in my life! I kept that vow for over ten years and I'm paying dearly for that now.

No matter how hard we try, no one will escape this appointment of judgment before God. *"For we must all appear before the judgment seat of Christ; that every one may receive the things done in his body, according to that he hath done, whether it be good or bad"* (2 Corinthians 5:10). Regardless of our status, John declares, *"I saw the dead, small and great, stand before God"* (Revelation 20:12). After 222 verses, Solomon, the wisest man to ever live, summarized it all with, *"Let us hear the conclusion of the whole matter: Fear God, and keep his commandments: for this is the whole duty of man. For God shall bring every work into judgment, with every secret thing, whether it be good, or whether it be evil"* (Ecclesiastes 12:13–14).

> *Forget the hype; forget the sensational; forget the emotional. There can be no change of heart without the piercing, penetrating and convicting power of the Word of God!*

The **Incredible Reality** is that no matter who we are or what we have done, whether saved or lost, we will meet God! What if it were today? As the old hymn says, would it be a "glad day"? I'm afraid for many, the words will have to change to "sad day." Take John's admonition, *"And now, little children abide in him; that, when he shall appear, we may have confidence, and not be ashamed before him at his coming"* (1 John 2:28).

God's Word Declares an Impenitent Rebellion

On occasion, in soulwinning, I have met someone who says, "I'm an atheist." I always respond, "God doesn't believe you." (It is fair. They don't believe in God, and He doesn't believe in them.) In all seriousness, there is no such thing as an atheist. *"For the invisible things of him from the creation of the world are clearly seen, being understood by the things that are made, even his eternal power and Godhead; so that they are without excuse"* (Romans 1:20). And according to chapter two in Romans, God has not only revealed Himself to every man, but has written His word on their hearts and consciences. *"Which shew the work of the law written in their hearts, their conscience also bearing witness, and their thoughts the mean while accusing or else excusing one another"* (Romans 2:15).

Yet in spite of this inner revelation from God, and the preaching of God's Word, there are many who still reject the message. *"And when they heard of the resurrection of the dead, some mocked: and others said, We will hear thee again of this matter"* (Acts 17:32). As Paul pleads with them to change their minds and turn to Christ, they turn away. Have you ever wondered why people reject God? Is it because they do not believe that He exists? Is it because they think the Bible is full of fairy tales and cannot be trusted? No. We have just seen from Romans 1–2 that every man knows there's a God, and His Word has been written on his heart. So why does he reject?

In his second letter, Peter is admonishing Christians to be mindful of the words they have heard before and hold on to them dearly. For he says, *"Knowing this first, that there shall come in the last days scoffers...."* What you have embraced as truth is going to come under attack. There will be those who scoff, ridicule, laugh at and reject this truth. Why? Because they don't believe in God or that His Word is true? No! Read the rest—*"...walking after their own lusts"* (2 Peter 3:3). There's the key. It's not that man does not believe God exists or that the Bible is a hoax; the problem is, he doesn't want to give up his sin! *"And this is the condemnation, that light is come into the world, and men loved darkness rather than light, because their deeds*

Someday you'll hear God's final call to you,
To take His offer of salvation true.
This could be it my friend, If you but knew
God's final call. God's final call.
If you reject God's final call of grace,
You'll have no chance your footsteps to retrace.
All hope will then be gone and doom you'll face
Oh hear His call. Oh hear His call.

---

were evil. For every one that doeth evil hateth the light, neither cometh to the light, lest his deeds should be reproved" (John 3:19–20).

When there is an **Impenitent Rebellion**:

God's Word Declares an Impending Removal

Be careful how you respond to the conviction of God's Word in your heart. There is a limit to God's grace. Oh, He loves you more than you can imagine and His longsuffering is more than any of us deserve, but there is a limit to His grace. *"The LORD is merciful and gracious, slow to anger, and plenteous in mercy. He will not always chide: neither will he keep his anger for ever"* (Psalm 103:8–9). While we love verse eight and rejoice that the Lord is a God of second chances, verse nine sternly reminds us that our opportunity to respond is limited. God told Noah to build an ark because He was going to destroy the world with water because of the wickedness that had come up before Him. Noah was instructed to preach on sin, righteousness, and judgment to come while he built the ark. But before he ever started, God had set the timetable of His grace, *"And the LORD said, My spirit shall not always strive with man, for that he also is flesh: yet his days shall be an hundred and twenty years"* (Genesis 6:3). Noah would faithfully preach and build. God's spirit would strive with men to repent. And for one hundred and twenty years men laughed and mocked the message. But when the time had expired, the door was shut by God and it began to rain!

Here on Mars' Hill, Paul faithfully declares God's Word. When that message was rejected, the Bible says, *"So Paul departed from among them"* (Acts 17:33). **Impenitent Rebellion** led to **Impending Removal.** Is God pleading with you today about your sinful life? Is He convicting you about the direction you are going and the way you are living? Thank God for that conviction and don't turn a deaf ear to that still small voice. He's speaking to you because He loves you and wants to make something of your life.

As a sophomore in high school, I had made the varsity football team. One day in practice I got my big break. The starting right guard, though an all-conference player on both sides of the ball, was having an awful practice. He had blocked the wrong player on three consecutive plays, and Coach Friedman, our fiery coach, had seen enough. He ordered Mike Uttech off the field and replaced him with Glenn Griebnow. I laughed as I watched Glenn make his way into that offensive huddle. He never knew what was going on and sure enough, he blocked the same guy Uttech had been blocking. Friedman literally picked him off the ground and threw him to the sideline. With his face bright red and the veins of his neck protruding outward, he marched over to where us scrubs were standing. He yelled, "Give me somebody! Give me anybody that can play that spot!"

I had been looking for a chance to play and so raced past him into that offensive huddle. I had memorized all of the blocking assignments in the playbook for all five line positions. There I was, in the huddle with my heroes! Big Frank Boling on one side at center, Cliff Roth the all-conference left tackle on the other side, and Jim Beaver our all-conference quarterback calling the play. As we broke the huddle, I reviewed my assignment in my mind. "Inside; outside; over; closest linebacker." It meant simply that when the ball was snapped, if there was a defensive player in my inside gap, he was mine to block. If there was no one in the inside gap, then I was to block the player in the outside gap. If no one was inside or outside, then I was to block the man over me. If no one was there, I was to block the closest linebacker. As Friedman used to say, "I don't care if the closest linebacker is sitting on the bench—GO BLOCK HIM!!"

The ball was snapped, and I nailed the defensive player creating a hole for the running back. The play went for fifteen yards, and I jumped to my feet knowing I had done a great job. But Friedman was already in my face, "WRONG, WRONG, WRONG—GET

OUT OF HERE!" I went to the sideline and stood next to Griebnow. Had it not been for my stubborn German pride I would have quit football that night. As I stood there, I felt an arm slip around my shoulder pads. I looked up, and it was big Cliff Roth, the senior left tackle. (Seniors didn't usually put their arms around sophomores!) He said, "John, what's the matter?" I said, "Cliff, you were in there. I blocked the right guy, and you know it. But Friedman climbed all over me." I'll never forget that big farm boy coming around and standing directly in front of me. He grabbed me by my facemask and with a jerk pulled it up next to his. With those beady eyes staring at me, he said, "John, as long as Friedman is yelling at you, he's trying to make you into a good football player. When he stops yelling, go hand in your stuff. He's given up!"

I learned something about football coaches that night and about my Heavenly Father. Oh, I'll be honest, it was humiliating when the coach would yell during those film sessions or throw a clipboard your way during halftime in frustration. But I would smile, because I knew he was still trying to make me into something. I watched the coach stop yelling at some guys and you know what? They never played again. He had given up.

Conviction is no fun, but when God's Word speaks, don't rebel. The worst thing that can happen to you is when that still small voice goes silent. Listen to the bone-chilling warning of Solomon:

> "How long, ye simple ones, will ye love simplicity? and
> the scorners delight in their scorning, and fools hate
> knowledge? Turn you at my reproof: behold, I will
> pour out my spirit unto you, I will make known my
> words unto you. Because I have called, and ye refused;
> I have stretched out my hand, and no man regarded;
> But ye have set at nought all my counsel, and would
> none of my reproof: I also will laugh at your calamity;
> I will mock when your fear cometh; When your fear
> cometh as desolation, and your destruction cometh

as a whirlwind; when distress and anguish cometh upon you. Then shall they call upon me, but I will not answer; they shall seek me early, but they shall not find me: For that they hated knowledge, and did not choose the fear of the LORD: *They would none of my counsel: they despised all my reproof. Therefore shall they eat the fruit of their own way, and be filled with their own devices. For the turning away of the simple shall slay them, and the prosperity of fools shall destroy them. But whoso hearkeneth unto me shall dwell safely, and shall be quiet from fear of evil.*
—PROVERBS 1:22–33

Study Questions

1. When a hot iron is placed on the flank of an animal, it hurts! But once the flesh has been "seared" with the hot iron, it is deadened to all feeling. Consider this illustration when you read 1 Timothy 4:1–2. What did Paul mean when he said, "…having their conscience seared with a hot iron"?

2. How does the Bible describe someone with a seared conscience? See Proverbs 29:1 and Ephesians 4:19.

3. Many times, the problem with someone who has a seared conscience is that he does not want to give up his sin. John 3:19 says, "…*men loved darkness rather than light, because their deeds were evil.*" God's Word has the ability to transform you, renew you, and change a seared conscience. Do you have any sin that you are holding onto right now to which your conscience has become deadened to over time?

4. Conviction from the Holy Spirit can be uncomfortable, but when God's Word speaks, listen. The worst thing that can happen to you is when that still small voice goes silent. Be honest with yourself and write briefly what the Holy Spirit has been convicting you about recently. If you can't think of anything, spend time in prayer asking God's Spirit to convict you of your sins.

5. Daniel Webster once said, "The greatest thought that can occupy a man's mind is his accountability to God." Write out the following verses that correspond with Daniel Webster's statement: Acts 17:31, Hebrews 9:27, and Amos 4:12.

Memory Verse

"*Let us hear the conclusion of the whole matter: Fear God, and keep his commandments: for this is the whole duty of man. For God shall bring every work into judgment, with every secret thing, whether it be good, or whether it be evil.*"—ECCLESIASTES 12:13–14

CHAPTER FOUR

The Realization of a Captured Mind

Howbeit certain men clave unto him, and believed: among the which was Dionysius the Areopagite, and a woman named Damaris, and others with them" (Acts 17:34). I like the way this chapter ends—on a positive note. While some hardened to the message of God, others heeded. Some mocked, but others melted.

God wants to capture our minds with truth. The world and all of its influences have been in control of our thoughts for too long. It's time to change our minds! It's time to bring *"into captivity every thought to the obedience of Christ"* (2 Corinthians 10:5). *"For to be carnally minded is death; but to be spiritually minded is life and peace"* (Romans 8:6).

The Captured Mind Begins with an Openness

When verse thirty-four speaks of some that "clave unto him" it means that they were open to the truth Paul was preaching. They were hungry and wanted more. What a joy to find people whose prayer is, *"Open thou mine eyes, that I may behold wondrous things out of thy law. I am a stranger in the earth: hide not thy commandments from me"* (Psalm 119:18–19). Is your mind open to God? Just prior to his visit to Mars' Hill, Paul had been with a group of people that he described as *"...more noble than those in Thessalonica, in that they received the word with **all readiness of mind**, and searched the scriptures daily, whether those things were so"* [Emphasis mine] (Acts 17:11).

The Captured Mind Proceeds with an Obedience

Not only did these in verse thirty-four cleave to Paul's words, but they "believed" (Acts 17:34). How precious the Word of God is when it is received with a desire to obey. *"As an earring of gold, and an ornament of fine gold, so is a wise reprover upon an obedient ear"* (Proverbs 25:12). The blessing of God rests on those who not only hear, but obey. *"But be ye doers of the word, and not hearers*

God isn't going to show you new truth until you obey the old truth.

only, deceiving your own selves. For if any be a hearer of the word, and not a doer, he is like unto a man beholding his natural face in a glass: For he beholdeth himself, and goeth his way, and straightway forgetteth what manner of man he was. But whoso looketh into the perfect law of liberty, and continueth therein, he being not a forgetful hearer, but a doer of the work, this man shall be blessed in his deed" (James 1:22–25).

Sometimes I hear people say, "God doesn't speak to my heart any more. Must be the preacher isn't doing his job, because God just doesn't speak to me." My friend, the problem is not with the preacher. The problem is, you didn't obey the last time He spoke. God isn't going to show you new truth until you obey the old truth. If I teach my grandkids to ride their bikes on the proper side of the road and they disobey me and ride wherever they want to, do you think I'm going to let them get behind the wheel of my car? God isn't going to show us the specifics of His Word and His will until we obey Him in the basics.

Have you obeyed the last message you heard? *"Therefore to him that knoweth to do good, and doeth it not, to him it is sin"* (James 4:17).

The Captured Mind Culminates in an Ownership

"...Among which was Dionysius the Areopagite, and a woman named Damaris, and others with them" (Acts 17:34). These two converts from the preaching on Mars' Hill did not seem that significant. They are certainly not household names of the faith. What is interesting however, is the last phrase, *"...and others with them."* Dionysius and Damaris **Opened** their minds to the truth, **Obeyed** that truth, and now **Owned** it in such a way as to make an impact on others.

When a "brainwash" truly takes place, this is exactly what happens. The Word of God changes the mind so the wrong thinking of the past is replaced by right thinking which affects the way that we live. Our minds affect our manners, remember? So if our manners are ever going to change, our minds have to be changed first. When right thinking takes place, right living will follow! Here's the way Joshua of old put it, *"This book of the law shall not depart out of thy mouth; but thou shalt meditate therein day and night, that thou mayest observe to do according to all that is written therein: for then thou shalt make thy way prosperous, and then thou shalt have good success"* (Joshua 1:8). Hearing God's Word causes us to meditate on it; which leads to the doing of it; which produces God's success! God's formula for a changed life starts with a changed mind.

Does God need to wash your brain out with soap? *"Now ye are clean through the word which I have spoken unto you"* (John 15:3). A lot of so-called "open minds" ought to be closed for cleaning! Your mind is a sacred enclosure into which nothing harmful can enter except by your permission. Why don't you give God permission today to wash it of the wrong thinking of the past and saturate it with the truth of His Word. *"Wherewithal shall a young man cleanse his way? by taking heed thereto according to thy word. With my whole heart have I sought thee: O let me not wander from thy commandments. Thy word have I hid in mine heart, that I might not sin against thee"* (Psalm 119:9–11).

> *A lot of so-called "open minds" ought to be closed for cleaning!*

When someone calls you one of those "brainwashed Christians," thank them for the compliment!

Study Questions

1. The captured mind begins with what?

2. Since we cannot wash our minds out with soap, how can we cleanse our minds? See John 15:3.

3. When right thinking takes place, right living will follow. Referencing Joshua 1:8, summarize the steps to right living and take special note of the first step.

4. Think back to the last spiritual truth you were taught and then read James 4:17. Have you obeyed that spiritual truth? What does the Bible say about knowing to do good and not doing it?

5. The blessing of God rests on those who not only hear, **but who also obey**. Write out what the Scriptures say about obedience in James 1:22–25.

Memory Verse

"Casting down imaginations, and every high thing that exalteth itself against the knowledge of God, and bringing into captivity every thought to the obedience of Christ;"—2 CORINTHIANS 10:5

PART TWO

Who Left the Brain-Door Open?

The routine was all too familiar—get up early, pack the van, drive most of the day, arrive at the next church, unpack, set up the display, sing and preach, fellowship, follow someone to his house, try to get some sleep in a strange bed only to get up the next day and do it all over again. Such is life on the road with a summer ensemble. But this night turned out to be very interesting! After the service, we were introduced to the family that would be keeping all of the girls in the group. I would follow the family out to their place, drop the girls off, and then they would give me directions to the motel where a room was waiting for me.

We wove our way into the beautiful Washington State countryside and arrived at the home of Mr. and Mrs. Baydo and their four daughters. As we approached the driveway, an electric gate opened and suddenly Mr. Baydo took off in the van! He was flying down the driveway toward the house. I was trying to keep up but soon thought better as horses began to scatter across their meticulously manicured front yard leaving deep holes with their hooves as they fled. As the van screeched to a stop, Mr. Baydo quickly jumped out and began chasing the horses back toward the corral, while yelling, "WHO LEFT THE GATE OPEN?!"

As I recall, no one ever admitted to being the culprit that night, but the damage had been done. The lawn—along with a lot of nerves—had been torn up that night because somebody left the gate open.

The child of God must be both open-minded and close-minded. That may seem like a contradiction, but let me explain. Mr. Baydo wouldn't be very smart if he built a corral without a gate. Indeed the corral would be closed all the time, but he also wouldn't be able to have any horses. There are times when the gate to the corral needs to be open. Feed needs to be taken into the corral; horses need to be led to and from for grooming and riding; the corral needs to be cleaned, etc. There are other times (particularly while you're at church) when the gate needs to be closed tightly.

Paul was concerned for the Christians trying to live for Christ in Rome. He knew that wicked influences were all around them, and he was concerned that those influences would enter their minds and corrupt them. Yet at the same time, he wanted them to be open to instruction from God and easily influenced to follow Him. He wrote, *"...I would have you wise unto that which is good, and simple concerning evil"* (Romans 16:19). The Apostle knew that they would have the blessing of God if they would follow the instruction in the very first Psalm, *"Blessed is the man that walketh not in the counsel of the ungodly, nor standeth in the way of sinners, nor sitteth in the seat of the scornful. But his delight is in the law of the LORD; and in his law doth he meditate day and night"* (Psalm 1:1–2).

How sad it is to see people (even God's people) who close their minds to truth and open it to sin and error. This problem is not new, for Jeremiah confronted it in his day, *"For my people is foolish, they have not known me; they are sottish children, and they have none understanding: they are wise to do evil, but to do good they have no knowledge"* (Jeremiah 4:22). How sad it is that many today know the latest fads and fashions, the top ten songs, Hollywood actors by name and movie, where to find pornography on the internet or corner store, but couldn't name the books of the Bible in order if you put a gun to their heads! What a sad culture indeed when we know more about evil than we do about good. The gates of our minds are wide open welcoming the pollution that destroys our lives and yet remain closed to "Thus saith the Lord."

Have you learned when to shut the brain-door? In Part One we discussed the importance of opening our minds to truth so that change in our minds can occur. Now we must discover the importance of being closed-minded. In 1 Timothy 4 we discover four reasons to keep the brain-door closed:

> *"Now the Spirit speaketh expressly, that in the latter times some shall depart from the faith, giving heed to seducing spirits, and the doctrines of devils; Speaking lies in hypocrisy; having their conscience seared with a hot iron; Forbidding to marry, and commanding to abstain from meats, which God hath created to be received with thanksgiving of them which believe and know the truth. For every creature of God is good, and nothing to be refused, if it be received with thanksgiving: For it is sanctified by the word of God and prayer. If thou put the brethren in remembrance of these things, thou shalt be a good minister of Jesus Christ, nourished up in the words of faith and of good doctrine, whereunto thou hast attained. But refuse profane and old wives' fables, and exercise thyself rather unto godliness. For bodily exercise profiteth little: but godliness is profitable unto all things, having promise of the life that now is, and of that which is to come. This is a faithful saying and worthy of all*

acceptation. For therefore we both labour and suffer reproach, because we trust in the living God, who is the Saviour of all men, specially of those that believe. These things command and teach. Let no man despise thy youth; but be thou an example of the believers, in word, in conversation, in charity, in spirit, in faith, in purity. Till I come, give attendance to reading, to exhortation, to doctrine. Neglect not the gift that is in thee, which was given thee by prophecy, with the laying on of the hands of the presbytery. Meditate upon these things; give thyself wholly to them; that thy profiting may appear to all. Take heed unto thyself, and unto the doctrine; continue in them: for in doing this thou shalt both save thyself, and them that hear thee."—1 TIMOTHY 4:1–16

Dead faith, seducing spirits, doctrines of devils, hypocritical lies, seared consciences, and old wives' fables dominate the thinking of man today. Timothy probably didn't need the history lesson any more than we do. There's a problem with the way we think because we have left our minds open to everything but truth. But Paul isn't preaching to the world now; he's done that (see Acts 20:31). In this letter, he is zeroing in on young Timothy, his son in the faith, admonishing him to guard the entrance to his mind. *"Keep thy heart with all diligence; for out of it are the issues of life"* (Proverbs 4:23).

CHAPTER FIVE

The Complacent Mind

Both the body and the brain have a tendency to be lazy! Our modern technology allows and encourages us to put our brains in neutral and let the television, the internet, the video game, or cell phone do the thinking for us. People boast of being broad-minded but are too lazy to think about what is right or wrong.

In Paul's second letter to Timothy, we get some insight into the aged apostle at the close of his life. He isn't sitting in a La-Z-Boy recliner enjoying his Social Security and planning his next trip to Maui. The frail aching body is hunched in the corner of a cold damp Roman prison awaiting execution. He expects any moment to hear the footsteps of the executioner who will lead him to the chopping block before Nero's throne. He is ready to be offered. These last two letters to young Timothy will enable him to carry the baton faithfully long after Paul is gone. As he shivers in the shadows of that lonely cell, he writes, *"The cloak that I left at Troas* with Carpus, when thou comest, bring with thee, and the books, but especially the parchments" (2 Timothy 4:13). In his dying moments he desires that the physical, mental, and spiritual all stay right. "My body is cold, so bring me my coat. My mind is weary, so bring me the books. My soul is hungry, so bring me the Scriptures." "I have a few more hours to use for Christ. This is no time to be complacent!" What a testimony! Nothing conceals your laurels so much as resting on them.

> **A lazy person tempts the devil to tempt him.**

Paul was practicing what he had preached. Here in 1 Timothy 4, he presents:

The Challenge of a Searching Mind

"Till I come, give attendance to reading" (1 Timothy 4:13). Statistics show that Americans spend more money annually on chewing gum than on books. (Thanks for buying this one and reading this far—may your kind increase!) But while reading is important, *what* you read is far more important. The information highway is cluttered with garbage and debris that is detouring many a life from God's destination for them.

I am amazed at how enamored we are with the wisdom of men and how bored we are with God's truth. We're all ears to the talking gurus of ESPN or FOX NEWS, but when our pastor stands to read Scripture, our minds wander and our attitude is, "I've heard all this before." *"For it is written, I will destroy the wisdom of the wise, and will bring to nothing the understanding of the prudent. Where is the wise? where is the scribe? where is the disputer of this world? hath not God made foolish the wisdom of this world?"* (1 Corinthians 1:19–20). No wonder we are in such a mess in this world. *"My people are destroyed for lack of knowledge: because thou hast rejected knowledge, I will also reject thee, that thou shalt be no priest to me: seeing thou hast forgotten the law of thy God, I will also forget thy children"* (Hosea 4:6).

The following was found written in the fly leaf of Evangelist Billy Sunday's Bible after he died:

> Twenty-nine years ago, with the Holy Spirit as my guide, I entered at the portico of Genesis, walked down the corridor of the Old Testament art galleries, where pictures of Noah, Abraham, Moses, Joseph, Isaac, Jacob, and Daniel hung on the wall. I passed into the music room of Psalms where the Spirit sweeps the keyboard of nature until it seems that every reed and pipe in God's great organ responds to the harp of David, the sweet singer of Israel.
>
> I entered the chamber of Ecclesiastes, where the voice of the preacher is heard, and into the conservatory of Sharon and the Lily of the Valley where sweet spices filled and perfumed my life.
>
> I entered the business office of Proverbs and on into the observatory of the prophets where I saw telescopes of various sizes pointing to far off events, concentrating on the bright and morning star which was to rise above the moonlit hills of Judea for our salvation and redemption.
>
> I entered the audience room of the King of Kings, catching a vision written by Matthew, Mark, Luke, and John. Thence into the correspondence room with Paul, Peter, James, and John writing the Epistles.
>
> I stepped into the throne room of Revelation where tower the glittering peaks, where sits the King of Kings upon His throne of glory with the healing of the nations in His hand, and I cried out…
>
> All hail the power of Jesus name!
> Let angels' prostrate fall;
> Bring forth the royal diadem
> And crown Him Lord of all.
>
> (W.A. Criswell, *Why I Preach the Bible is Literally True*, Broadman Press, 1969)

I wonder does that describe your Bible reading this morning? Or did you just check off a box on a Bible reading schedule? God commands us to *"Study to shew thyself approved unto God, a workman that needeth not to be ashamed, rightly dividing the word of truth"* (2 Timothy 2:15). Jesus said, *"Search the scriptures; for in them ye think ye have eternal life: and they are they which testify of me"* (John 5:39). The gems of Scripture are not all found on the surface. They must be mined by a diligent search. *"My son, if thou wilt receive my words, and hide my commandments with thee; So that thou incline thine ear unto wisdom, and apply thine heart to understanding; Yea, if thou criest after knowledge, and liftest up thy voice for understanding; If thou seekest her as silver, and searchest for her as for hid treasures; Then shalt thou understand the fear of the LORD, and find the knowledge of God"* (Proverbs 2:1–5).

The Challenge of a Stirred Mind

"Till I come, give attendance to…exhortation" (1 Timothy 4:13). The faithful preaching and teaching of God's Word is designed to stir our minds. The Apostle Peter wrote his second Epistle for this very purpose, *"This second epistle, beloved, I now write unto you; in both **which I stir up your pure minds** by way of remembrance"* [Emphasis mine] (2 Peter 3:1). Peter's audience had heard the truth many times before, but it was his desire to keep preaching it so that their minds would be established in truth. *"Wherefore I will not be negligent to put you always in remembrance of these things, though ye know them, and be established in the present truth. Yea, I think it meet, as long as I am in this tabernacle, to stir you up by putting you in remembrance"* (2 Peter 1:12–13).

Today people think they have "killed the fatted calf" if they go to church on Sunday morning. In the Book of Acts, the people went every day. Maybe that's why the early church was seeing constant revival and we are not. *"Not forsaking the assembling of ourselves together, as the manner of some is; but exhorting one another: and so much the more, as ye see the day approaching"* (Hebrews 10:25). Jeremiah said, *"My people have committed two evils; they have forsaken me the fountain of living waters, and hewed them out cisterns, broken cisterns, that can hold no water"* (Jeremiah 2:13). The parking lots of stadiums, movie houses, bars, and shopping malls are packed daily as we fill our lives with all that the well of the world has to offer, while there are pews at the front of the church

> **One truth from the Bible is worth more than all the wisdom of man.**

that have not been sat on in years. No wonder our minds resemble cesspools rather than fountains of truth.

You say, "I don't like preaching; it makes me uncomfortable." It's supposed to! It is designed by God to stir up our minds. God's Word comforts the distressed but also distresses the comfortable. *"Take heed, brethren, lest there be in any of you an evil heart of unbelief, in departing from the living God. But exhort one another daily, while it is called To day; lest any of you be hardened through the deceitfulness of sin"* (Hebrews 3:12–13). In a world that daily numbs our minds into believing a lie, we need the exhortation of God's Word to stir us up to truth.

The Challenge of a Sound Mind

"Till I come, give attendance to...doctrine" (1 Timothy 4:13). Paul exhorted Timothy *"to stir up the gift which is in thee"* and then in the next verse reminded him, *"For God hath not given us the spirit of fear: but of power, and of love, and of **a sound mind**"* [Emphasis mine] (2 Timothy 1:6–7). A mind that **Searches** the Scriptures and is constantly **Stirred** up through the preaching of those Scriptures, will be a **Sound** mind.

People go through life seeking peace and contentment. They try all that the devil has to offer, but nothing satisfies. From party to party and weekend to weekend they are left empty with a craving for more of that which never satisfies. *"The wicked are like the troubled sea, when it cannot rest, whose waters cast up mire and dirt. There is no peace, saith my God, to the wicked"* (Isaiah 57:20–21). Above the din of the world, Jesus calls, *"Come unto me, all ye that labour and are heavy laden, and I will give you rest. Take my yoke upon you,* and **learn of me**; *for I am meek and lowly in heart: and ye shall find rest unto your souls. For my yoke is easy, and my burden is light"* [Emphasis mine] (Matthew 11:28–30). *"Thou wilt keep him in perfect peace, **whose mind is stayed** on thee: because he trusteth in thee. Trust ye in the* LORD *for ever: for in the* LORD JEHOVAH *is everlasting strength"* [Emphasis mine] (Isaiah 26:3–4).

> **Stop reading your Bible, and let the Bible start reading you!**

Don't let your mind become complacent. *"Blessed are they which do hunger and thirst after righteousness: for they shall be filled"* (Matthew 5:6). Job said, *"Neither have I gone back from the commandment of his lips; I have esteemed the words of his mouth more than my necessary food"* (Job 23:12). Have *you* eaten today?

Study Questions

1. First Timothy 4:13 says to give attendance to what three things?

2. What two evils did the people commit in Jeremiah 2:13?

3. Describe your Bible reading. Is it beneficial, consistent, thorough, and applicable to your daily life? After referring to John 5:39 and 2 Timothy 2:15, how can you enhance your time spent in the Bible?

4. In your own words, explain how this statement is true: "A lazy person tempts the devil to tempt him."

5. God's Word comforts the distressed and distresses the comfortable. We need the exhortation of God's Word to stir us up to truth. Write the following verses regarding biblical exhortation: Hebrews 3:12–13.

Memory Verse

"Blessed are they which do hunger and thirst after righteousness: for they shall be filled."—MATTHEW 5:6

CHAPTER SIX

The Careless Mind

The Danish philosopher, Soren Kierkegaard told the following parable which illustrates what happens when we become careless. "One day a duck was flying with his mates in the springtime northward across Europe. During the flight he came down in a Danish barnyard where there were tame ducks. He enjoyed some of their corn. He stayed for an hour, then for a day, then for a week, then for a month, and finally, because he relished the good fare and the safety of the barnyard, he stayed all summer. But one autumn day when the flock of wild ducks were winging their way southward again, they passed over the barnyard, and their mate heard their cries. He was stirred with a strange thrill of joy and delight, and with a great flapping of wings he rose in the air to join his old comrades in their flight.

"But he found that his good fare had made him so soft and heavy that he could rise no higher than the eaves of the barn. So he dropped back again to the barnyard, and said to himself, 'Oh well, my life is safe here and the food is good.' Every spring and autumn when he heard the wild ducks honking, his eyes would gleam for a moment, and he would begin to flap his wings. But finally the day came when the wild ducks flew over him and uttered their cry, but he paid not the slightest attention to them" (Clarence Macartney, *Preaching without Notes*, Abingdon Press, 1937).

Because our minds are capable of receiving and processing and then storing tons of information daily, a careless attitude toward our thoughts is devastating. Here in 1 Timothy, Paul is challenging the life of young Timothy and says, *"Meditate upon these things"* (1 Timothy 4:15). To the Philippians, Paul said, *"Think on these things."* What things? *"Those things, which ye have both learned, and received, and heard, and seen in me…"* (Philippians 4:8–9). The challenge is to discipline our thoughts in the right direction so that we can live the right result. *"I thought on my ways, and turned my feet unto thy testimonies"* [Emphasis mine] (Psalm 119:59).

So how do we counteract **A Careless Mind**?

A Cultivation of Truth

"Neglect not the gift that is in thee, which was given thee by prophecy, with the laying on of the hands of the presbytery" (1 Timothy 4:14). Paul had gone to a lot of trouble to mentor Timothy in the truth of God's Word. The responsibility was now Timothy's. He could neglect what had been sown in his heart and let the thorns of life choke the Word, or he could cultivate the soil of his heart so that the truth could grow and mature to a wonderful harvest.

There was not a more boring job on the farm than cultivating corn. I enjoyed driving tractors from the time I was a little boy. (They were less complicated and easier to drive in those days.) Like all boys, I love going fast! To get out on the road and do fifteen or twenty miles an hour on a tractor is pretty exhilarating for a little kid! Cultivating corn however, was just the opposite—slow and boring. When the corn was just coming up out of the ground, you had to slowly move through those rows with the cultivator lest you throw dirt on the tiny plants and crush them. But while cultivating corn was tedious it was extremely important. If weeds were allowed to take over, there would be no crop in October.

Each week your pastor, Sunday school teacher, and perhaps others prepare and then sow truth in your heart through preaching and teaching. Each day as you read the Bible personally, the Holy Spirit guides you into the truth of God's Word. But what are *you* doing with that seed? There are 168 hours in every week. Let's see, if you spend three hours in church and another seven hours reading your Bible (an hour a day would be extreme for most people), that means you are receiving truth ten hours each week. That means the devil has 158 hours to sow weeds! I think we'd better do some cultivating or the truth is going to die.

> ***The sermon that pricks the conscience has good points.***

The prophets of the Old Testament understood the need to cultivate the heart. Jeremiah cried, "*Break up your fallow ground*" (Jeremiah 4:3). Hosea preached, "*Sow to yourselves in righteousness, reap in mercy; break up your fallow ground: for it is time to seek the* LORD, *till he come and rain righteousness upon you*" (Hosea 10:12).

It is our responsibility to keep our hearts as "good ground" where the truth can flourish and produce God-honoring results. Don't just "check off" your Bible reading each day and "do church" on Sundays. The Apostle Peter had invested his life in the ministry of helping others follow Christ. Notice his parting words:

> "*Wherefore, beloved, seeing that ye look for such things, be diligent that ye may be found of him in peace, without spot, and blameless. And account that the longsuffering of our Lord is salvation; even as our beloved brother Paul also according to the wisdom given unto him hath written unto you; As also in all his epistles, speaking in them of these things; in which are some things hard*

to be understood, which they that are unlearned and unstable wrest, as they do also the other scriptures, unto their own destruction. Ye therefore, beloved, seeing ye know these things before, beware lest ye also, being led away with the error of the wicked, fall from your own stedfastness. But grow in grace, and in the knowledge of our Lord and Saviour Jesus Christ. To him be glory both now and for ever. Amen."—2 PETER 3:14–18

Growth does not come without **A Cultivation of Truth.**

A Contemplation of Truth

"Meditate upon these things" (1 Timothy 4:15). Meditation is a lost art. We have too much to *do* to think. Henry Ford said, "Thinking is the hardest work there is, which is probably the reason so few people engage in it." The little prefix "I think" is probably the most over-exaggerated expression of the English language! Amazingly, we spend time thinking about wrong things, but rarely contemplate truth. *"Stand in awe, and sin not: commune with your own heart upon your bed, and be still"* (Psalm 4:4).

Growing up on a farm, I learned early in life about the digestive process of cows. A cow can eat an enormous amount of food very quickly. (I would get up every morning before daylight and go out and chop an entire wagon full of alfalfa for them to eat, only to come home from school and have to do it again. In the winter, I would feed each cow a wheelbarrow full of fodder twice a day, which they would devour in about five minutes!) After eating, however, the cow goes through an unusual process. Their food goes down into the first of four stomachs and then is ruminated a little at a time.

> *Most folks have presence of mind. The trouble is absence of thought.*
> —Howard W. Newton

Contentedly, the cow "chews her cud" for hours as the food is chewed between stomachs.

While that process in cows is not the most pleasant to ponder, it is this same process that God wants us to have with His Word. *"This book of the law shall not depart out of thy mouth; but **thou shalt meditate therein day and night...**"* [Emphasis mine] (Joshua 1:8). Have you "chewed" on any truth lately?

If we are going to "chew" on truth all day, it makes sense to get that truth into our lives early in the day. *"O God, thou art my God; early will I seek thee: my soul thirsteth for thee, my flesh longeth for thee in a dry and thirsty land, where no water is"* (Psalm 63:1). Reading and memorizing God's Word early in the day will allow you to "think" on it throughout the day. By the way, the "earlier" a child comes to Christ and is taught to read his Bible the better. Those early truths engrained upon their minds will come back in times of decision and difficulty.

> ***Don't just take notes, study them! There will be a test.***

There are many things in life that, when we think about them, bring distress, discouragement, and disaster. A meditation on God's Word will do just the opposite. *"But his delight is in the law of the LORD; and in his law doth he meditate day and night"* (Psalm 1:2). God's Word will direct your thoughts toward the Lord and *"My meditation of him shall be sweet: I will be glad in the LORD"* (Psalm 104:34).

A Consumption with Truth

"...give thyself wholly to them; that thy profiting may appear to all" (1 Timothy 4:15). D. L. Moody said, "I never saw a useful Christian who was not a student of the Bible." Jeremiah was obviously consumed with God's Word, *"Thy words were found, and I did eat them; and thy word was unto me the joy and rejoicing of mine heart: for I am called by thy name, O LORD God of hosts"* (Jeremiah 15:16). The

psalmist likewise expresses his joy in God's Word, *"And I will delight myself in thy commandments, which I have loved"* (Psalm 119:47). *"The law of thy mouth is better unto me than thousands of gold and silver"* (Psalm 119:72). *"O how I love thy law! it is my meditation all the day"* (Psalm 119:97). *"Thy word is very pure: therefore thy servant loveth it"* (Psalm 119:140).

Charles Spurgeon once said, "You should spend so much time in the Bible that your language become Bibline." I don't think "Bibline" is a word, but I believe I know what he means. It wouldn't hurt for a "thee" and a "thou" to slip out once in awhile. It would be better than what often slips out now!

Izaak Walton said of his Bible, "Every hour I read you, kills a sin, or lets a virtue in to fight against it." Don't let your mind become **A Complacent Mind** or **A Careless Mind**. Fill it with the Truth! Because if you don't, you will be dealing with a big problem. Keep reading to find out just how big.

Study Questions

1. Philippians 4:8 tells us to think on which things?

2. Reading and memorizing God's Word early in the day will allow you to "think" on it throughout the day. List two Scriptures that support this truth.

3. D.L. Moody said, "I never saw a useful Christian who was not a student of the Bible." Do you consider yourself a student of the Bible? Explain your answer.

4. You are to discipline your thoughts in the right direction so that you can live the right way. Psalm 119:59 says, *"I thought on my ways, and turned my feet unto thy testimonies."* Think on your ways, and determine whether you need to turn back to God's Word. What changes do you need to make?

5. The prophets of the Old Testament understood the need to cultivate the heart. Write out their exhortations in Jeremiah 4:3 and Hosea 10:12.

Memory Verse

"This book of the law shall not depart out of thy mouth; but thou shalt meditate therein day and night, that thou mayest observe to do according to all that is written therein: for then thou shalt make thy way prosperous, and then thou shalt have good success."—JOSHUA 1:8

CHAPTER SEVEN

The Contaminated Mind

P aul now warns Timothy, *"Take heed unto thyself, and unto the doctrine; continue in them: for in doing this thou shalt both save thyself, and them that hear thee"* (1 Timothy 4:16). **A Complacent Mind** and **A Careless Mind** will lead to **A Contaminated Mind**. Therefore, "take heed!" Keep the brain-door closed to the wrong influences.

A Closed Brain-Door Will Keep Your Vessel Clean

"Take heed unto thyself..." (1 Timothy 4:16). God commands us to take the water of life to this world. That water, however, needs to flow through a clean conduit. Unfortunately, you cannot separate the message from the messenger. The right content and the right conduit are equally important. Have you ever drunk water out of a garden hose? I remember vividly the first time I did so. What a

horrible taste and smell! Now there's nothing wrong with the water. You could go over to that outside faucet and fill a glass with water and not think anything of it. But there's something that changes drastically when that water flows through that old garden hose.

There is nothing wrong with the truth that God has given to us. The water of life is exactly what every person in this world needs. The problem is, God has chosen that it flow through us. That's going to require a clean conduit. "...*Let every one that nameth the name of Christ depart from iniquity. But in a great house there are not only vessels of gold and of silver, but also of wood and of earth; and some to honour, and some to dishonour. If a man therefore purge himself from these, he shall be a vessel unto honour, sanctified, and meet for the master's use, and prepared unto every good work*" (2 Timothy 2:19–21).

My family and I have enjoyed owning a few dogs over the years. While we always tried to take good care of them and provide good food and fresh water, I was never once tempted to eat or drink out of the dog's dish! Oh, it was a nice one—two compartments; sky

---

THY WORD

Thy Word is like a garden, Lord, with flowers bright and fair;
And every one who seeks may pluck a lovely cluster there.
Thy Word is like a deep, deep mine; and jewels rich and rare
Are hidden in its mighty depths for every searcher there.
Thy Word is like a starry host, a thousand rays of light
Are seen to guide the traveler, and make his pathway bright.
Thy Word is like an armory, where soldiers may repair,
And find for life's long battle-day all needful weapons there.
Oh, may I love Thy precious Word; may I explore the mine;
May I its fragrant flowers glean; may light upon me shine.
Oh, may I find my armor there; Thy Word my trusty sword,
I'll learn to fight with every foe the battle of the Lord.
—EDWIN HODDER, SOURCEBOOK OF POETRY

---

blue in color; we probably paid all of $2.95 for it at Wal Mart—but no matter how thirsty I was, never one time did I ever get down on my hands and knees and start drinking. I'm sure you understand. While the dog's dish is a vessel, it is a dishonorable one and no one in his right mind would take in even clean water from such a source. No one wants truth coming from an error-filled life either. Keeping our thoughts right will keep our vessel clean.

A Closed Brain-Door Will Keep Your Values Centered

"Take heed...unto the doctrine" (1 Timothy 4:16). Interestingly, Paul first addresses the conduit, but now stresses the content. It's not only sin that can ruin our thinking, but also the false teachings that constantly swirl around us. By keeping your mind in the Word of God, you will be able to ferret out those things that are contrary to truth. Solomon put it succinctly in the proverb, *"The thoughts of the righteous are right: but the counsels of the wicked are deceit"* (Proverbs 12:5). You won't fall to the counsels of deceit if your thoughts are right.

Now be careful, because the Bible teaches us that our own hearts are deceitful. *"The heart is deceitful above all things, and desperately wicked: who can know it"* (Jeremiah 17:9). Because we can't trust ourselves to think right, we must saturate ourselves with the truth that God has given us. *"But strong meat belongeth to them that are of full age, even those who by reason of use have their senses exercised to discern both good and evil"* (Hebrews 5:14). That's why God gave it to us. *"Whereby are given unto us exceeding great and precious promises: that by these ye might be partakers of the divine nature, having escaped the corruption that is in the world through lust"* (2 Peter 1:4).

When God's Word is *valuable,* your *values* will be right. Notice how those two concepts were interwoven in the psalmist's life:

"O how love I thy law! it is my meditation all the day. Thou through thy commandments hast made me wiser than mine enemies: for they are ever with me. I have more understanding than all my teachers: for thy testimonies are my meditation. I understand more than the ancients, because I keep thy precepts. I have refrained my feet from every evil way, that I might keep thy word. I have not departed from thy judgments: for thou hast taught me. How sweet are thy words unto my taste! yea, sweeter than honey to my mouth! Through thy precepts I get understanding: therefore I hate every false way. Thy word is a lamp unto my feet, and a light unto my path. I have sworn, and I will perform it, that I will keep thy righteous judgments."—PSALM 119:97–106

A Closed Brain-Door Keeps Your Voice Clear

"...for in doing this thou shalt both save thyself, and them that hear thee" (1 Timothy 4:16). When you are thinking purely, you never have to worry about speaking dirty. The old computer saying, "Garbage in—Garbage out" is also true of the mind. *"Either make the tree good, and his fruit good; or else make the tree corrupt, and his fruit corrupt: for the tree is known by his fruit. O generation of vipers, how can ye, being evil, speak good things? for out of the abundance of the heart the mouth speaketh. A good man out of the good treasure of the heart bringeth forth good things: and an evil man out of the evil treasure bringeth forth evil things"* (Matthew 12:33–35).

It was said of Jesus, *"Never man spake like this man"* (John 7:46). Why was this said? Because *"...in him is no sin"* (1 John 3:5). All of us have said things that we regret. Perhaps in frustration you have said, "Why did I say that?" But way before we stop our tongues, we must stop our thoughts. It works the other way too. When we are thinking right, the right words will come when we need them.

Have you ever been witnessing to someone and later were amazed that you thought of certain verses to use? God allowed you to speak what you had stored!

Keep the brain-door closed so as to prevent **A Complacent Mind, A Careless Mind,** and **A Contaminated Mind**. In the early verses of 1 Timothy chapter four, Paul is very specific about why it is so important to keep **A Closed Mind**. With ten-thousand thoughts going through our brain waves a day, it's awfully easy for the wrong things to slip in. Let's look at some of these specific reasons for:

Study Questions

1. What are the three benefits of having a closed brain-door?

2. God has chosen that His Word should flow through you, and He requires that it flow through a clean conduit. What steps can you take in your life to make yourself a clean conduit for God's truth?

3. According to Jeremiah 17:9, can we trust the thoughts in our hearts?

4. When God's Word is valuable to you, your values will be right. Refer to Psalm 119:97–106 and explain how this concept directed the psalmist's life.

5. All of us have said things that we regret. Perhaps in frustration you have said, "Why did I say that?" But way before we stop our tongue, we must stop our thoughts. Write out Matthew 12:33–35 to help you think before you speak.

Memory Verse

"The thoughts of the righteous are right: but the counsels of the wicked are deceit."—Proverbs 12:5

CHAPTER EIGHT

The Closed Mind

A Closed Mind Guards against Heretical Deception

"Now the Spirit speaketh expressly, that in the latter times some shall depart from the faith, giving heed to seducing spirits, and the doctrines of devils" (1 Timothy 4:1). The devil never stops attacking. He is on a mission that will not end until he is cast into the Lake of Fire for eternity. *"But evil men and seducers shall wax worse and worse, deceiving, and being deceived. But continue thou in the things which thou hast learned and hast been assured of, knowing of whom thou hast learned them"* (2 Timothy 3:13–14).

The devil has an arsenal full of weapons. He will use *accusation*. John wrote, *"And I heard a loud voice saying in heaven, Now is come salvation, and strength, and the kingdom of our God, and the power of his Christ: for the accuser of our brethren is cast down, which accused them before our God day and night"* (Revelation 12:10). He will use *opposition.* That's why Peter said, *"Be sober, be vigilant; because your adversary the devil, as a roaring lion, walketh about, seeking whom he may devour"* (1 Peter 5:8). He will use *imitation.* He tried that with Jesus when he said, *"All these things will I give thee, if thou wilt fall down and worship me"* (Matthew 4:9).

But no doubt, Satan's number one weapon is *deception.* *"And the great dragon was cast out, that old serpent, called the Devil, and Satan, which deceiveth the whole world"* (Revelation 12:9). The devil loves deceiving people about immorality, drugs, or alcohol. He has even deceived people about death, as many people think if they commit suicide "they will end it all." But he saves his most sophisticated deception for the spiritual. How many people around the world are deceived about eternal life? What they believe sounds so right. How could something that my church teaches, or that my parents taught me, or that so many people believe, possibly be wrong? *"For such are false apostles, deceitful workers, transforming themselves into the apostles of Christ. And no marvel; for Satan himself is transformed into an angel of light. Therefore it is no great thing if his ministers also be transformed as the ministers of righteousness; whose end shall be according to their works"* (2 Corinthians 11:13–15). The devil's best work is done by those who claim to know God.

> ***Nothing can "slip out" that first didn't "slip in."***

Years ago in a revival meeting, a young couple that had been newly saved informed their pastor that the Jehovah Witnesses were coming by their home for Bible studies every week. They had not asked them to come; they just showed up, and the young couple didn't want to tell someone who was so "religious" that they weren't welcome. The pastor was very upset that this was happening to these new converts but really didn't know what to tell them. I asked when they normally came, and they told me it was the same time each week. I said, "Well, why don't you invite the pastor and me to come over about that time?"

They were more than happy to have us come, and so we arrived about fifteen minutes before the regular time. Sure enough, they knocked on the door, and the young couple immediately invited them in and introduced them to us. (Of course, we did not reveal we were Baptist preachers.) They started their usual Bible study, and we all listened intently. The young couple kept glancing at us as if to say, "See, this is good—it's all about the Bible."

After about an hour, I was getting weary of their deception and so asked the man, "Do you believe that Jesus Christ was the Son of God and that the only way to Heaven is through Him?" He said, "No," and then tried to explain. As soon as he said "no," the young Christian jumped to his feet and said, "What! You don't believe that Jesus was God! What are you going to teach me if you don't even believe in my Saviour? I'm sorry, you're going to have to leave NOW!"

It's fun to expose error with truth and that is exactly what the Apostle John instructed us to do.

> *"Beloved, believe not every spirit, but try the spirits whether they are of God: because many false prophets are gone out into the world. Hereby know ye the Spirit of God: Every spirit that confesseth that Jesus Christ is come in the flesh is of God: And every spirit that confesseth not that Jesus Christ is come in the flesh is not of God: and this is that spirit of antichrist, whereof ye have heard that it should come; and even now already is it in the world. Ye are of God, little children, and have overcome them: because greater is he that is in you, than he that is in the world. They are of the world: therefore speak they of the world, and the world heareth them. We are of God: he that knoweth God heareth us; he that is not of God heareth not us. Hereby know we the spirit of truth, and the spirit of error."*—1 JOHN 4:1–6

A Closed Mind Guards against Hypocritical Demands

"Speaking lies in hypocrisy; having their conscience seared with a hot iron; Forbidding to marry, and commanding to abstain from meats..." (1 Timothy 4:2–3). It is amazing what people believe that cannot be backed up by the Book. People will go to great lengths to find a solution for the sin problem, but totally ignore what the Bible says. There is a man over in the Philippines who allows himself to be crucified on a cross every year in order to try to pay for his sins. It reminds me of Naaman in the Old Testament who was prepared to give ten talents of silver, a thousand pieces of gold, and ten changes of raiment to the man who could heal him of his leprosy. When Elisha's messenger told him to wash in the Jordan, he got mad and stomped out. Thank God for his servants who reasoned with him, *"My father, if the prophet had bid thee do some great thing, wouldest thou not have done it? how much rather then, when he saith to thee, Wash, and be clean? Then went he down, and dipped himself seven times in Jordan, according to the saying of the man of God: and his flesh came again like unto the flesh of a little child, and he was clean"* (2 Kings 5:13–14).

People say, "God told me," or "the Holy Spirit spoke to me." Be careful! God isn't going to contradict His Word. The Holy Spirit will never tell you anything that is not in the Holy Scriptures. *"Howbeit when he, the Spirit of truth, is come, he will guide you into all truth: for he shall not speak of himself; but whatsoever he shall hear, that shall he speak: and he will shew you things to come"* (John 16:13).

In his letter to the Corinthians, Paul made sure that his hearers knew that he was not preaching his opinions or ideas. He didn't want their wisdom to be based on his enticing words or excellent speech, but on the very Word of God. He reminds them that the Holy Spirit will always confirm in their hearts what the Bible teaches. *"But God hath revealed them unto us by his Spirit: for the Spirit searcheth all things, yea, the deep things of God. For what man knoweth the things of a man, save the spirit of man which is in him? even so the things of God knoweth no man, but the Spirit of God. Now we have received, not the spirit of the world, but the spirit which is of God; that we might know the things that are freely given to us of God. Which things also we speak, not in the words which man's wisdom teacheth, but which the Holy Ghost teacheth: comparing spiritual things with spiritual"* (1 Corinthians 2:10–13).

We must guard our minds against any teaching that makes demands not found in God's Word. *"Every word of God is pure: he is a shield unto them that put their trust in him. Add thou not unto his words, lest he reprove thee, and thou be found a liar"* (Proverbs 30:5–6). R. A. Torrey said, "God's Word is pure and sure, in spite of the devil, in spite of your fear, in spite of everything."

A Closed Mind Guards against Hopeless Diversions

"But refuse profane and old wives' fables, and exercise thyself rather unto godliness" (1 Timothy 4:7). A good rule is: If it doesn't *edify—eliminate!* *"Neither give heed to fables and endless genealogies, which minister questions, rather than godly edifying which is in faith: so do"* (1 Timothy 1:4). Some people are well-versed in nothingness. Good things can even keep us from the best things. *"All things are lawful unto me, but all things are not expedient: all things are lawful for me, but I will not be brought under the power of any"* (1 Corinthians 6:12).

> ***The Bible sure throws a lot of light on the Bible commentaries.***
> ***—Barnhouse***

I have often asked myself as I start a day or a week, "What on my 'to do list' will make it into eternity?" Destinations are never reached by taking exits. I love the single-mindedness of Paul, *"And now, behold, I go bound in the spirit unto Jerusalem, not knowing the things that shall befall me there: Save that the Holy Ghost witnesseth in every city, saying that bonds and afflictions abide me. But none of these things move me, neither count I my life dear unto myself, so that I might finish my course with joy, and the ministry, which I have received of the Lord Jesus, to testify the gospel of the grace of God"* (Acts 20:22–24). Too often we have more than "one thing" that is "needful."

A Closed Mind Guards against Hindered Diligence

"...and exercise thyself rather unto godliness. For bodily exercise profiteth little: but godliness is profitable unto all things, having promise of the life that now is, and of that which is to come" (1 Timothy 4:7–8). How's your exercise program? While physical exercise profits for life, spiritual exercise profits for life and eternity. I have been jogging since 1985. Most days I get five miles in and I believe overall it is profitable. In more recent years, I have mixed in some cycling to keep my body fooled! While not a body-builder by any stretch, I endeavor to lift some weights regularly to keep up some level of strength. I have missed exercising some days to be sure over the years due to travel or other circumstances, but I honestly don't remember the last day I missed reading my Bible. I can think of once or twice when I went out for a run *before* I read my Bible and I regretted it all day. I never want my physical exercise to become my god, but I sure want the Bible to be my guide.

It is amazing how diligent and disciplined we can be in areas of little importance. We just have to watch the big game, watch the news, go to work, eat lunch, work out, etc., but how diligent are we in godliness? *"And herein do I exercise myself, to have always a conscience void of offence toward God, and toward men"* (Acts 24:16).

A Closed Mind Guards against Harmful Departure

The apostle shares his heart in the very first verse of this chapter we have studied, *"...in the latter times some shall depart from the faith*" (1 Timothy 4:1). I wonder how many Christians would still be ministering if they had guarded their minds? There are no sadder phrases in Scripture than, *"For Demas hath forsaken me"* (2 Timothy 4:10), *"...thou hast left thy first love"* (Revelation 2:4), or *"For some are already turned aside after Satan"* (1 Timothy 5:15). You depend on God, but can He depend on you? In God's book of remembrance, I think *faithful* and *famous* are the same word.

It's not just our lives that are on the line here. Sure, we can make our own choices and live with the consequences, but what about others who are watching? In the last verse of this chapter, as Paul reminds Timothy to *"take heed"* and *"continue"* he says, *"...for in doing this thou shalt both save thyself,* **and them that hear thee**" [Emphasis mine] (1 Timothy 4:16). I have often thought that when we get to Heaven we will be surprised at the number of people who are there *because* of us. Think about it: Have you ever prayed for people to be saved? Have you ever given money to missions? Have you ever handed out a Gospel tract? Have you ever witnessed to someone? We don't get to see most of the results of those efforts, but God takes it all and uses it *"precept upon precept; line upon line...here a little, and there a little"* to bring people to Himself (Isaiah 28:10). I dare say that all of us will meet people in Heaven who are there in some way *because* of us.

But will there be anyone in Hell *because* of us? That is a much more sobering question. Sadly, Paul wrote to the church at Rome, *"For the name of God is blasphemed among the Gentiles through you..."* (Romans 2:24). He told the Corinthian church, *"Awake to righteousness, and sin not; for some have not the knowledge of God: I speak this to your shame"* (1 Corinthians 15:34). What a tragedy that we fail to keep the wrong thoughts from our minds and as a result someone else misses Heaven!

It was a busy summer day on the farm—they always are. It was harvest time and hundreds of bales of hay needed to be brought in. "Making hay when the sun shines" is a motto well known to the diligent farmer! But just as we headed to the fields, word came that the cows were out!

We pastured our cows across the river on some rented land. Mom had gotten a phone call from some neighbors that our cows were running across their corn fields and they were not happy. We abandoned our task of baling hay and drove as fast as we could to the pasture. Being on the other side of the river, we had to drive several miles to get there and when we did, the cows were everywhere and enjoying every minute of this new found freedom.

Once out of a pasture, cows can get very disoriented. For the next several hours we chased cows! In the midst of it all, I got stung on the top of my head by a bumble bee. My dad was running cows down from seemingly all over the county; my mom was running back home to get ice for my head, and I was bawling my eyes out. I was just a kid, but I'll never forget that day. Yes, it was I who left the gate open. My dad never spanked me for my negligence. I guess he figured the bee had inflicted enough pain. People were frustrated, cows were injured, milk production was down for the next two days, and part of the harvest was lost all because I didn't close the gate!

The world crowns success; God crowns faithfulness.

Your mind is the gateway to your heart. Guard what goes in and out.

Study Questions

1. We must guard our minds against heretical deception. How can we do this according to 1 John 4:1–6?

2. Good things can keep us from the best things. First Corinthians 6:12 says, *"All things are lawful unto me, but all things are not expedient: all things are lawful for me, but I will not be brought under the power of any."* As you review your priorities in life, do you see any areas where something good takes first over that which is best?

3. Look at your "to-do" list this week. Make a list of items from your "to-do" list that will last for eternity. What items can you add to next week's "to-do" list that will have more of an impact on eternity?

5. We must guard our minds against any teaching that makes demands not found in God's Word. In light of this principle, write out Proverbs 30:5–6.

Memory Verse

"Be sober, be vigilant; because your adversary the devil, as a roaring lion, walketh about, seeking whom he may devour:"—1 PETER 5:8

3

PART THREE

Mind Control

Critics of biblical Christianity have often accused us of having a "flock-like" mentality. We are branded as being cultish and under some kind of "mind-control." Neo-orthodoxy was founded by Karl Barth (1896–1968) which paved the way for existentialism, that is, each individual creating truth from his own experiences rather than following the absolute Word of God. Barth attacked fundamentalists (those who believe the Bible literally) by accusing them of worshipping a "paper pope."

So what's wrong with being controlled by truth? Are we so foolish as to trust our own experience rather than "Thus saith the Lord"? Remember, we have hearts that are *deceitful above all things, and desperately wicked* (Jeremiah 17:9). We may *think* we are right in our own eyes but the plumb line of God's Word will not lead us astray. *"For we can do nothing against the truth, but for the truth"* (2 Corinthians 13:8).

A story is told of the captain of a ship who looked out one night into the darkness and saw a light directly in their path. He instructed his signalman to send a message, "Alter your course ten degrees north." Soon a reply came, "Alter *your* course ten degrees south." The captain was not happy—his message had been ignored. He sent a second, "Alter your course ten degrees north. I am a Captain!" The reply came, "Alter *your* course ten degrees south. I am 3ʳᵈ Class Seaman Jones." The captain was outraged. He sent a third message knowing the fear it would evoke, "Alter your course ten degrees north. I am a battleship!" The response came, "Alter *your* course ten degrees south. I am a lighthouse!"

We can resist and reject the truth, but it will still be true. Your obstinate will is never going to change God's omniscient will. When Jesus prayed for us, He said, *"Sanctify them through thy truth: thy word is truth"* (John 17:17). God never has and never will lie! *"God is not a man, that he should lie; neither the son of man, that he should repent: hath he said, and shall he not do it? or hath he spoken, and shall he not make it good?"* (Numbers 23:19). In fact, the writer of Hebrews declares that it is *"impossible for God to lie"* (Hebrews 6:18).

How we need a generation of people today who will not ignore the truth of God's Word, but rather be impacted by that truth. *"If ye continue in my word, then are ye my disciples indeed; And ye shall know the truth, and the truth shall make you free"* (John 8:31b–32). Every child of God has the opportunity and ability to understand the truth of God's Word because *"...when he, the Spirit of truth, is come, he will guide you into all truth"* (John 16:13). Do you have the desire to be guided into the Truth? Wouldn't you like your entire life to be under the control of the Truth?

"Mind Control?" Why not? We are all being influenced by something. I like the results of being influenced by the Spirit much better than the results of being influenced by the flesh. *"Know ye not, that to whom ye yield yourselves servants to obey, his servants ye are to whom ye obey; whether of sin unto death, or of obedience unto righteousness? But God be thanked, that ye were the servants of sin, but ye have obeyed from the heart that form of doctrine which was delivered you. Being then made free from sin, ye became the servants of righteousness"* (Romans 6:16–18).

In Ephesians chapter four, there are several aspects of a mind controlled by truth:

"And he gave some, apostles; and some, prophets; and some, evangelists; and some, pastors and teachers; For the perfecting of the saints, for the work of the ministry, for the edifying of the body of Christ: Till we all come in the unity of the faith, and of the knowledge of the Son of God, unto a perfect man, unto the measure of the stature of the fullness of Christ: That we henceforth be no more children, tossed to and fro, and carried about with every wind of doctrine, by the sleight of men, and cunning craftiness, whereby they lie in wait to deceive; But speaking the truth in love, may grow up into him in all things, which is the head, even Christ: From whom the whole body fitly joined together and compacted by that which every joint supplieth, according to the effectual working in the measure of every part, maketh increase of the body unto the edifying of itself in love. This I say therefore, and testify in the Lord, that ye henceforth walk not as other Gentiles walk, in the vanity of their mind, Having the understanding darkened, being alienated from the life of God through the ignorance that is in them, because of the blindness of their heart: Who being past feeling have given themselves over unto lasciviousness, to work all uncleanness with greediness. But ye have not so learned Christ; If so be that ye have heard him, and have been taught by him,

as the truth is in Jesus: That ye put off concerning the former conversation the old man, which is corrupt according to the deceitful lusts; And be renewed in the spirit of your mind; And that ye put on the new man, which after God is created in righteousness and true holiness."—EPHESIANS 4:11–24

CHAPTER NINE

Guided by A Censored Mind

God desires that the Holy Spirit serve as a censor or filter to our minds so that the things of this world are not able to enter. *"And be not conformed to this world: but be ye transformed by the **renewing of your mind**, that ye may prove what is that good, and acceptable, and perfect, will of God"* [Emphasis mine] (Romans 12:2). This continual process of filtering makes it possible for us to be *"wise unto that which is good, and simple concerning evil"* (Romans 16:19). How can we have this censored mind?

Through the Gift of Called Men

In verse eleven, God lists for us the human gifts to the local church. *"And he gave some, apostles; and some, prophets; and some, evangelists; and some, pastors and teachers"* (Ephesians 4:11). The twelve *apostles* were the first to follow Christ in His ministry and were later designated as such because they were eyewitnesses of His life after the resurrection (see Acts 1:22). This gift is no longer in existence today because the qualification of being an eyewitness is impossible. Likewise, the *prophets* as listed here are no longer needed because the canon of Scripture is complete.

However, the office of the evangelist and pastor/teacher is still very functional and important today in the local church. Those who preach faithfully the truth of God's Word are given to us as a gift from God to help us have censored minds. Just because you have been disappointed by a preacher or two, don't "throw out the baby with the bathwater." There may be some hypocrites in the pulpit just as there are in the pew, but don't let that dissuade you from the truth that comes to you through the preaching of these God-called men.

I have never met anyone who was living a successful Christian life who was not a part of a local church where the Word of God was being preached faithfully. And I'm not sure that I ever will because God "*hath in due times manifested his word through preaching*" (Titus 1:3). God doesn't need us to build the church, but we sure need the church to build our lives. "*For the preaching of the cross is to them that perish foolishness; but unto us which are saved it is the power of God*" (1 Corinthians 1:18). God has called men to preach and commanded us to submit to the authority of that truth. "*Remember them which have the rule over you, who have spoken unto you the word of God: whose faith follow, considering the end of their conversation*" (Hebrews 13:7).

One day, at the judgment, each preacher will give an account of his faithfulness to preach the truth, and every person who has heard that truth will give an account of his obedience to that Word. "*Obey them that have the rule over you, and submit yourselves: for they watch for your souls, as they that must give account, that they may do it with joy, and not with grief: for that is unprofitable for you*" (Hebrews 13:17). How sad it is that many people today find excuses week after week to miss preaching services in their churches and then wonder why their minds are stained with worldly thoughts. *"Now ye are clean through the word which I have spoken unto you"* (John 15:3).

Through the Goal of Christ-like Maturity

Why did God give us these human gifts (the evangelist and pastor/teacher)? Paul answers that:

> *"For the perfecting of the saints, for the work of the ministry, for the edifying of the body of Christ: Till we all come in the unity of the faith, and of the knowledge of the Son of God, unto a perfect man, unto the measure of the stature of the fullness of Christ: That we henceforth be no more children, tossed to and fro, and carried about with every wind of doctrine, by the sleight of men, and cunning craftiness, whereby they lie in wait to deceive; But speaking the truth in love, may grow up into him in all things, which is the head, even Christ: From whom the whole body fitly joined together and compacted by that which every joint supplieth, according to the effectual working in the measure of every part, maketh increase of the body unto the edifying of itself in love."*
> —EPHESIANS 4:12–16

God wants us to become like Him. If that is going to take place, we must filter out that which doesn't assist in that goal. *"For whom he did foreknow, he also did predestinate to be conformed to the image of his Son"* (Romans 8:29A). In a very general sense, there are three stages in God's plan for our lives. There is **salvation** which takes place the moment you put your faith and trust in Jesus Christ. There is **sanctification** which begins the moment you get saved and doesn't end until **glorification** when we are with the Lord and then are like Him.

Salvation   **Sanctification**   **Glorification**

If you are a child of God, you are today in the stage of **sanctification** somewhere between **salvation** and **glorification**. If we could picture you on a timeline, are you closer to **salvation** or are you closer to **glorification**? Many people take just a few tiny baby steps after they get saved. The distance between them and the world is minimal. Others, because they place their minds under the control of the Spirit of God and His Word, grow by leaps and bounds placing great difference between them and the world. When they die or Jesus comes, their step into **glorification** will be minimal for they have already grown to be like Him.

Using God's Word as the measuring stick, are you closer to **salvation** or **glorification**? *"As obedient children, not fashioning yourselves according to the former lusts in your ignorance: But as he which hath called you is holy, so be ye holy in all manner of conversation; Because it is written, Be ye holy; for I am holy"* (1 Peter 1:14–16). Let's grow up and act our age! Many have been saved for years and yet still act like "babes in Christ."

No wonder that the world goes on lost in their sin—they see no difference in those who profess to be different! If God has changed your *destiny*, then let Him change your *demeanor*, so that others can see Christ in you. *"But ye are a chosen generation, a royal priesthood, an holy nation, a peculiar people; that ye should shew forth the praises of him who hath called you out of darkness into his marvelous light: Which in time past were not a people, but are now the people of God: which had not obtained mercy, but now have obtained mercy. Dearly beloved, I beseech you as strangers and pilgrims, abstain from fleshly lusts, which war against the soul; Having your conversation honest among the Gentiles: that, whereas they speak against you as evildoers, they may by your good works, which they shall behold, glorify God in the day of visitation"* (1 Peter 2:9–12).

Through the Grieving over Corrupted Morality

When light is turned out, darkness prevails. When a person closes his eyes to the truth of God's Word, no light can enter his heart. As a result he is forced to walk in "the vanity of his mind." *"This I say therefore, and testify in the Lord, that ye henceforth walk not as other Gentiles walk, in the vanity of their mind, Having the understanding darkened, being alienated from the life of God through the ignorance that is in them, because of the blindness of their heart"* (Ephesians 4:17–18).

I was speaking at a Christian school one morning for chapel. After the invitation at the close of the service, a group of five or six teenagers came up onto the platform to ask me a question. I placed my Bible back on the pulpit and began to talk with these young people. As I did, I noticed there was a young man standing at the foot of the stairs leading up to the platform who was also waiting to speak with me. It was obvious that he was a bit perturbed that others had beaten him to me, as he was now showing his impatience by making funny noises of disdain. Finally, after a few moments of answering questions, the teens made their way off the platform and headed to class. The young man waited until they had completely exited the auditorium and then stomped his foot on every stair on his way up to me.

When he arrived at the pulpit, he threw up his hands and said, "Problems, problems, problems!" I thought, what kind of a nut is this? I looked at him and said, "Son, I don't want to hear any problems." He looked at me rather surprised. Preachers are supposed to listen to problems, but quite honestly, I didn't feel like it. Instead, I asked him, "Are you saved?" He said, "Of course, I'm saved!" I said, "Do you read your Bible every day?" Disgustedly, he said, "No." I said, "Was there ever a time in your life when you read the Bible every day?" He thought a moment and said, "Yeah, about two years ago, I read it every day." I looked into his eyes and asked,

"When did your problems start?" He paused and his head dropped. When he looked up, there were tears in his eyes, as he said, "About two years ago."

I put my arm around him and said, "I don't know what it is that's bugging you today, but that is your *problem.*" Jesus declared, *"Ye do err, not knowing the scriptures"* (Matthew 22:29A). Life is going to be filled with all kinds of problems when our minds are not being censored on a regular basis by the truth of God's Word. Are you reading God's Word daily? Are you in church when the doors are open listening to God's Word being preached? How do we expect to "walk as children of light" when we are doing nothing to dispel the darkness? We must be guided by a **Censored Mind**.

Study Questions

1. We are to protect our minds with the help of authority God has placed over us. According to Hebrews 13:7 and 17, how are we to respond to our authority?

2. According to Titus 1:3, through what does God manifest His Word?

3. To have minds that are Christ-like and mature, we must be a student of the gifts God has given to us. The Apostle Paul answers the question, "Why did God give us human gifts?" Read Ephesians 4:12–16 and summarize his answer.

4. In a very general sense, there are three stages in God's plan for our lives. The first stage is salvation, which takes place the moment you put your faith and trust in Jesus Christ. List and describe the other two stages.

5. Write out Ephesians 4:17–18—a passage of Scripture which admonishes us not to walk in vanity or corrupt morality.

Memory Verse

"And be not conformed to this world: but be ye transformed by the renewing of your mind, that ye may prove what is that good, and acceptable, and perfect, will of God."—ROMANS 12:2

CHAPTER TEN

Guided by a Clean Mind

When we ask Christ into our lives to save us, the Bible declares that *"...if any man be in Christ, he is a new creature: old things are passed away; behold, all things are become new"* (2 Corinthians 5:17). That being true, how does sin creep back into our lives as children of God? We know that we cannot lose our salvation, for Jesus declared, *"And I give unto them eternal life; and they shall never perish, neither shall any man pluck them out of my hand. My Father, which gave them me, is greater than all; and no man is able to pluck them out of my Father's hand"* (John 10:28–29).

Ephesians 4:19–20 gives us the process whereby we allow sin into our minds. Many a mother, after giving her little boy a bath, has said, "Now stay clean!" Mom wants him to be clean in the worst way for church or some other important function. But little boys are little boys and dirt has a way of presenting itself. When God cleansed us from sin at salvation, He desires that we stay clean. But sin has a way of presenting itself and that attack always begins in the mind.

An Insensitive Conscience

"Who being past feeling..." (Ephesians 4:19A). Watch out when you no longer sense the Spirit of God speaking to you through His Word! Remember what we said earlier about the brand on the flank of the cow? Like many a branded animal, we must not allow our conscience to be *"seared with a hot iron"* (1 Timothy 4:2). God had a message for the prophet Jeremiah to deliver to the nation of Israel, *"Declare this in the house of Jacob, and publish it in Judah, saying, Hear now this, O foolish people, and without understanding; which have eyes, and see not; which have ears, and hear not; Fear ye not me? saith the LORD: will ye not tremble at my presence?"* (Jeremiah 5:20–22). By the time we get to chapter eight of Jeremiah, this seared conscience led to a sorry condition, *"Were they ashamed when they had committed abomination? nay, they were not at all ashamed, neither could they blush: therefore shall they fall among them that fall: in the time of their visitation they shall be cast down, saith the LORD"* (Jeremiah 8:12).

Dr. Paul Brand was a physician who did much to advance the treatment of leprosy. As he lived among the lepers to study them and treat them, he would regularly take baths in scalding water. His purpose in this was to discover if there were any parts of his body where he might have lost feeling. He knew that if there was any part of his body that had lost sensitivity to the boiling water, it was there that the leprosy had attacked him (Gordon MacDonald, *A Resilient Life*, Nashville: Nelson Books, 2004, p. 17).

> *Conscience is a small voice deep down inside where the acoustics are generally poor.*

So, where has your life become insensitive? Do we still blush at a curse word or immoral scene on television? Are we still appalled by a lie? Does bitterness or pride bother us or has it become our pet sin? Christians today are allowing words, thoughts, music, friends, entertainment, etc., into their lives that would have bothered their conscience a few years ago. Conscience is that thing that hurts when everything else feels good. Cultivate a clear conscience; it may turn out to be the best friend you ever had. The polluting of our minds begins with an **Insensitive Conscience**.

An Invited Corruption

"…have given themselves over unto lasciviousness" (Ephesians 4:19). Once the conscience is seared, it is easy to plunge forward into wrong thinking. The door into our minds has been cracked open, and sin just automatically thinks it has been invited inside. It is amazing how you can't just sin a little. Sin never stays little; it always grows. That little sin in our minds can grow until it causes our whole life's direction to change.

Recently, I had my first experience with a kidney stone. I went to bed as normal on a Saturday night after driving most of the day to get to a church so that I could preach the services the next morning. About ten minutes into sleep, I was awakened by an intense pain in my abdomen. I tried everything over the next two hours to rid myself of that horrible pain, but nothing worked. After arriving at an emergency room in a strange town, they put me on some morphine and did a CAT scan. Five hours later, I was given the news: You have a kidney stone—textbook symptoms—you should pass it in the next few hours. As the doctor was sending me home, he instructed me to try to "catch" the stone so that they could study it and find out its cause. As he handed me a "strainer," I asked him what I was looking for? He said, "Oh, you won't be impressed—it's about the size of a grain of sand." I had heard that the pain of passing a kidney stone was like having a baby. I thought, "a grain of sand?" I'm about to deliver a world-class midget! How could such a little thing create so much torment?

Like that grain of sand creating such an intense pain, when we open our minds' door to the thought of sin, we are asking for big problems. No wonder Paul was so emphatic! *"But put ye on the Lord Jesus Christ, and make not provision for the flesh, to fulfil the lusts thereof"* (Romans 13:14). *"Neither give place to the devil"* (Ephesians 4:27). Solomon in his wisdom warned, *"My son, if sinners entice thee, consent thou not"* (Proverbs 1:10). Evangelist Billy Sunday used to say, "If you don't want to sin, stay out of the devil's neighborhood." There is way too much window-shopping at the mall of sin. Only fools fool with sin. Flirting with temptation always leads to romance with sin.

An Increased Continuation

"...to work all uncleanness" (Ephesians 4:19c). Like a cancer, sin begins to work its way into every part of our lives. Adam and Eve allowed a *doubt* and ended up in *disobedience.* Lot allowed a *division* and ended up in *drunkenness.* Achan allowed *covetousness* and ended up in a *cemetery.* Samson allowed a *look* and ended up in *lust.* David started out *missing from battle,* and ended up *murdering in brutality.*

"But every man is tempted, when he is drawn away of his own lust, and enticed. Then when lust hath conceived, it bringeth forth sin: and sin, when it is finished, bringeth forth death" (James 1:14–15). No sin starts with murder, or rape, or robbery. It begins with a thought and grows into an action.

Have you ever gone early to a major league baseball game? After the teams take a couple of hours of batting and infield practice, the field is cleared so that the grounds crew can ready the field for play. Every person on the field over the next few minutes has a job to do—some are watering down the infield while others are putting new bases in place. Usually, one man works alone around home plate. His job is to carefully re-chalk the batter's box. Two boxes are neatly placed on both sides of the plate. To stand outside of these boxes while hitting is illegal, and so they are meticulously measured and chalked.

When "Play Ball!" is heard echoing from the home plate umpire, the first batter steps to the plate. If you watch, his first move is to try to erase the back of the batter's box with his spikes. He deletes that clearly marked line by mixing the chalk with dirt until it is hardly discernible. Now with the line no longer clear, he "cheats" back in the box as far as he can without being called out, so as to see the pitch for as long as possible.

God went to a lot of trouble to give us His clearly defined commandments. How casually we rub them out and rationalize that we are "close" to the "batter's box" of His Word. Edmund Burke writes, "The instances are exceeding rare of man immediately passing over a clear marked line from virtue into declared vice and corruption. There are middle tints and shades between the two extremes; there is something uncertain on the confines of the two empires which they must pass through, and which renders the change easy and imperceptible" (George Sweeting, *Who Said That?*, Chicago: Moody Press, 1994, p. 117).

David never dreamed he would commit murder after such a track record of victory, but the problem with a little sin is that it never stays little.

An Inflamed Clamoring

"...*with greediness*" (Ephesians 4:19D). The fire of sin is hard to put out! The devil has plenty of fuel to throw on that fire to keep it burning for a long time. When I was a teenager, I took care of a cemetery. There was a lot of brush in the fence line, and so my Dad and I spent several days clearing out all of the vines and thorns that had grown into the fence. After several days, we had quite a pile of brush across the road from the cemetery down in a ravine.

A few days later, my Dad told me to ride my bike over there and burn that pile of brush. I took some matches and made my way eagerly to the ravine. This was going to be fantastic fire, and I was looking forward to watching the inferno. I lit a couple of small twigs at the bottom of that brush pile, but they would burn for just a few seconds and then go out. I found some old newspaper and tried lighting it, but the same thing happened. Those stumps and branches were just too "green" to burn, so I decided to add some "fuel to the fire."

I walked over to the little storage shed that we had at the cemetery and got a large ten-gallon drum of gasoline. My theory was actually pretty good, but my methods were flawed. I again lit some newspaper and got it burning at the bottom of the pile. I stood back a few feet and took the drum of gasoline and with the lid open, I clumsily slung some gasoline toward the fire. I don't remember much about the next few seconds. An inferno would be an understatement as the flames shot up not only from the brush pile but from the ten-gallon drum that I was still holding! I threw that drum into the fire and ran. When I heard the explosion of that drum I dove to the ground, covered my head and hoped that none of the shrapnel from that exploding drum would fall on me.

Allow a little sin into your mind and the devil will be sure to add the fuel to that sin. Within a very short time, you will have a fire of sin burning in your life that will be difficult to extinguish. We can get to the point where we enjoy the sin that we once abhorred. "*Who knowing the judgment of God, that they which commit such things are worthy of death, not only do the same, but have pleasure in them that do them*" (Romans 1:32). Your appetite for sin will increase more and more. "*...the mouth of fools feedeth on foolishness*" (Proverbs 15:14). Sin that was once feared is now commonplace. "*How much more abominable and filthy is man, which drinketh iniquity like water?*" (Job 15:16). Doing wrong is now as normal as getting a drink of water.

This **Insensitive Conscience, Invited Corruption, Increased Continuation**, and **Inflamed Clamoring** is all a result of:

An Ignored Communication

"But ye have not so learned Christ" (Ephesians 4:20). Paul reminds us that we did not learn this wrong pattern from Christ. All through the process of closing our minds to God, the Holy Spirit tries to warn us. Are you ignoring God's warnings today? *"…because when I called, ye did not answer; when I spake, ye did not hear; but did evil before mine eyes, and did choose that wherein I delighted not"* (Isaiah 65:12). It's one thing to ignore the counsel of good people in your life, but to turn a deaf ear to God is a very dangerous trend. *"He that hath an ear, let him hear…"* (Revelation 2:29). The saddest places in the Bible are the times when the voice of God is ignored. *"O Jerusalem, Jerusalem, thou that killest the prophets, and stonest them which are sent unto thee, how often would I have gathered thy children together, even as a hen gathereth her chickens under her wings, and ye would not"* (Matthew 23:37).

When I first started out in Evangelism, my family and I traveled in a Chevy Suburban and pulled a twenty-five foot Airstream trailer. Having grown up on a farm, I never struggled with some of the challenges of pulling that trailer that some of my fellow-evangelists did. But on one particular occasion, my over-confidence got me into trouble.

I was preaching for the Dublin Christian Academy in Dublin, New Hampshire for a school revival. Their academy is located on the top of a New England mountain, and it was December. We got our trailer up there without any problems and enjoyed being on the campus for the various chapels that took place during the day. In the evenings, we would drive down the mountain and over to the town of Peterborough where we would hold revival services for a new church plant at the Town Hall.

As Friday approached, I began to do some planning for our departure. We were scheduled to begin meetings in Pittsburgh on Sunday, and the forecast there in New Hampshire was for freezing temperatures with some rain or snow. Since we would need to leave after the service on Friday night in order to make it to Pittsburgh by Sunday, I decided to hook up the trailer after the last chapel and take it down the mountain before the temperatures dropped below freezing. I knew that winding road down the mountain would get icy as the temperature dropped. The pastor and his family had invited us to eat at their house at five, and so I had planned to drive into town and park the trailer in one of the store parking lots near the Town Hall and walk to the pastor's house.

Everything worked fine as we made it down the mountain and into town without any problems. But as I got to the main street of town, it suddenly dawned on me that it was Friday night during the Christmas season and all of the stores were open until late. Thus, all of the parking lots were full, and there was no place to park our rig. By now it was dark and close to five o'clock, but I knew that I had no choice but to go back out to the highway and circle back over the mountain to the pastor's home. This was the day prior to cell phones, and I didn't want to be late to the pastor's home. I knew that we were about fifteen minutes away if all went well, but it was nearing five o'clock.

As I drove down the main street, I remembered that there was a one-lane road that went over the mountain and came out about a block from the pastor's house. We had driven it one day as we were out soulwinning. I remembered that it was the road right after the Public Library. As I approached that corner, I told my family that I knew a shortcut. Immediately, I sensed the Holy Spirit saying, "Don't do it!" I rounded the corner anyway and pressed the accelerator down in order to gain some speed up this incline that was probably about a half mile in distance.

The Holy Spirit kept saying, "Stop! Don't do this! Turn around now!" But I ignored that voice. That 454 Chevy engine was roaring now as we chugged toward the top. About twenty yards from the crest, my rear wheels began to spin on the icy pavement below. (It was colder near the top and the moisture on the road had frozen.) No problem, I thought. I put my foot on the brake and allowed a few seconds to pass, knowing from experience that the heat of my spinning tires would melt the ice beneath them and we would be able to move forward momentarily. As I took my foot off of the brake and applied the accelerator however, we began to slide backwards. As I hit the brake, the truck and trailer began to jackknife. When I would let off the brake, I could straighten the rig slightly, but as soon as I would hit the brake again we would jackknife and slide a little closer to the edge of that one-lane road.

On the passenger side, where my wife was sitting, there was a deep ravine that plunged about five hundred feet down with a few young pine trees that wouldn't have held a snowmobile on that mountain much less a twenty-thousand pound rig! On my side there was a deep ditch of about fifty feet that didn't look any more inviting. At one point, I decided to set the parking brake and get out and take a look at our situation since it was by now completely dark. As I got out of the truck however, it began to slide past me, so jumping back in I announced to my family, "WE ARE GOING TO DIE!"

We managed to slip and slide backwards down that mountain about a hundred yards when my wife informed me that if we slid any closer to the edge on her side, we were going over. I again made sure that everybody in the truck knew that they were saved, we said our prayers, and I decided to take my foot off of the brake, close my eyes, and hope for the best. Because of our jackknifed position, the trailer pulled our truck off of the road to the left where there "just so happened" to be a driveway that we hit dead center and plunged into a giant bank of snow backwards!

It took awhile to shovel out the back of that trailer from the snow, but we were able to pull out of that driveway and head back down the mountain and to the pastor's house. (We were only about an hour late for dinner, but I wasn't very hungry anyway.) I don't think that still small voice ever stopped talking until we got to Pittsburgh Saturday night! He just kept saying, "I told you so!" What's that voice telling you today? Don't ignore His communication.

Study Questions

1. When we open our mind's door to the thought of sin, we are asking for big problems. The following Scriptures contain warnings about sin. Look up the following verses and write a sentence summarizing each verse: Romans 13:14, Ephesians 4:27, and Proverbs 1:10.

2. In the battle of trying to keep our minds clean from sin, the devil tries to create an appetite for sin. What do the following verses say about having an appetite for sin: Proverbs 15:44 and Job 15:16?

3. Through the process of closing our minds to God, the Holy Spirit tries to warn us. Are you ignoring God's warnings today? Does Isaiah 65:12 describe your response to God's warnings? Explain your answer.

4. Describe the last time you sensed God's Holy Spirit leading you. What was He asking, and how did you respond?

5. Sin begins with a thought and grows into an action. Write out James 1:14–15—the Bible's clear process of sin.

Memory Verse

"Therefore if any man be in Christ, he is a new creature: old things are passed away; behold, all things are become new."
—2 CORINTHIANS 5:17

CHAPTER ELEVEN

Guided by a Conformed Mind

We are never going to be able to think right on our own. *"Not that we are sufficient of ourselves to think any thing as of ourselves; but our sufficiency is of God"* (2 Corinthians 3:5). Our minds must be conformed to God's mind if we are going to please Him. That has been God's desire since the day He saved us, *"For whom he did foreknow, he also did predestinate to be conformed to the image of his Son…"* (Romans 8:29). In these next few verses of Ephesians four, Paul gives us three practical steps to take if we are going to have minds that are conformed to Christ.

Repent of Sinful Patterns

"That ye put off concerning the former conversation the old man, which is corrupt according to the deceitful lusts" (Ephesians 4:22). Put off! Get rid of! Repent! Change your mind! *"Repent therefore of this thy*

*wickedness, and pray God, if perhaps the **thought of thine heart** may be forgiven thee"* [Emphasis mine] (Acts 8:22).

Have you ever noticed that we have a certain pattern of thought? It seems that some thoughts, no matter how hard we try to ignore them, continue to return. Sometimes these thoughts are resurrected from our lives before we were saved. Notice Paul speaks of the "former conversation" or the "unsaved mind." He also tells us to rid our minds of that which is "corrupt" in this verse. That would speak of the "unholy mind"—those things that we have allowed in as sinful thought patterns. Then he says we must turn from "deceitful lusts" which speak of the thoughts that have been entertained by an "unbridled mind." The unsaved mind, the unholy mind, and the unbridled mind, must all be acknowledged as wrong sinful patterns, and repentance is necessary to rid the mind of these sinful patterns.

We often repent of sinful actions because they are seen and get us into trouble. But have you ever repented of sinful thought patterns? We often have to apologize for yelling at our children because we didn't deal with the anger that was welling up in our hearts. Repenting of the patterns of selfishness, pride, bitterness, unforgiveness, covetousness, jealousy, envy, and lust will save you from dealing with sinful actions later. *"For as he thinketh in his heart, so is he…"* (Proverbs 23:7).

There was a commercial on television years ago for Fram oil filters. It showed an auto mechanic looking under the hood of a car with a smoking engine. Someone had failed to change his oil regularly and now his engine needed to be replaced—a very expensive proposition. The old mechanic would hold up the advertised oil filter and say, "You can pay me now, or you can pay me later." Repenting of sinful patterns is a price that must be paid now or we will pay dearly later.

Resist with Spirit-filled Power

"And be renewed in the spirit of your mind" (Ephesians 4:23). The human spirit fails unless the Holy Spirit fills. D. L. Moody said, "God commands us to be filled with the Spirit; and if we aren't filled, it's because we are living beneath our privileges." You and I are not going to win this battle of our minds without the power of the Holy Spirit. As long as we think that we can think right on our own, we think wrong! *"…This is the word of the LORD unto Zerubbabel, saying, Not by might, nor by power, but by my spirit, saith the LORD of hosts"* (Zechariah 4:6). *"Now unto him that is able to do exceeding abundantly above all that we ask or think, according to the power that worketh in us"* (Ephesians 3:20).

Now in order to be filled, I must be empty. The gas tank on my car is always full. But while it is always full, I may come to a complete stop along side of the road because of a lack of fuel. Let me explain: My tank is always full of something—either air or gasoline. Unfortunately, cars do not run on air so we must keep them filled with fuel. When you put gasoline into your car, you are forcing the air in that tank out. This same principle applies to our lives. When we are filled with self, the Holy Spirit is forced out, but when we empty ourselves of ourselves and the sinful patterns that accompany our sinful selves, and are filled with the Spirit of God, we will have thoughts and actions that are pleasing to God. John put it succinctly, *"He must increase, but I must decrease"* (John 3:30).

The analogy that the Bible uses in Ephesians chapter five is interesting. *"And be not drunk with wine, wherein is excess; but be filled with the Spirit"* (Ephesians 5:18). When a person is drunk with alcohol, there is no question that he is "under the influence" of that which he has placed within him. He may try to cover up that influence, but he can't. Ask him to walk a straight line—he can't. Ask him to repeat the alphabet—he can't. His words are slurred, his mind is slowed, his movements are awkward, all because he cannot control himself. He is under the control of something else.

When we are empty of our own sinful patterns of thought and our minds are controlled by the Holy Spirit, it will likewise be undeniable. We can't hide it. It's obvious as our speech, our actions, and even our reactions are now controlled by the Spirit of God rather than our sinful flesh. Have you **Repented of Sinful Patterns** and are you **Resisting with Spirit-filled Power**? Martin Luther said that God made the world out of nothing, and it is only when we become nothing that God can make something out of us.

Replace with Scriptural Precepts

"And that ye put on the new man, which after God is created in righteousness and true holiness" (Ephesians 4:24). The "replacement theory" as I like to call it, is found throughout the Bible. Putting off, that is repentance, is a huge first step in the process, but the wrong must be replaced by that which is right if victory is to be secured.

Notice several places where God emphasizes replacement:

> *"Blessed is the man that walketh not in the counsel of the ungodly, nor standeth in the way of sinners, nor sitteth in the seat of the scornful. But his delight is in the law of the LORD; and in his law doth he meditate day and night."*—PSALM 1:1–2

> *"Let him that stole steal no more: but rather let him labour, working with his hands the thing which is good, that he may have to give to him that needeth."*—EPHESIANS 4:28

> *"Let love be without dissimulation. Abhor that which is evil; cleave to that which is good. Be kindly affectioned one to another with brotherly love; in honour preferring one another; Not slothful in business; fervent in spirit; serving the Lord; Rejoicing in hope; patient in tribulation; continuing instant in*

prayer; Distributing to the necessity of saints; given to hospitality. Bless them which persecute you: bless and curse not. Rejoice with them that do rejoice, and weep with them that weep. Be of the same mind one toward another. Mind not high things, but condescend to men of low estate. Be not wise in your own conceits. Recompense to no man evil for evil. Provide things honest in the sight of all men. If it be possible, as much as lieth in you, live peaceably with all men. Dearly beloved, avenge not yourselves, but rather give place unto wrath: for it is written, Vengeance is mine; I will repay, saith the Lord. Therefore if thine enemy hunger, feed him; if he thirst give him drink: for in so doing thou shalt heap coals of fire on his head. Be not overcome with evil, but overcome evil with good."
—Romans 12:9–21

Paul sums it up nicely later, *"But now ye also put off all these; anger, wrath, malice, blasphemy, filthy communication out of your mouth. Lie not one to another, seeing that ye have put off the old man with his deeds; And have put on the new man, which is renewed in knowledge after the image of him that created him"* (Colossians 3:8–10). The old simply must be replaced by the new!

You say, "But I've been thinking wrong for so long; I just don't think I can change the way I think. I've tried to quit the wrong thought patterns. I've been to the altar and confessed them. They just keep coming back." Let's try an experiment. Think of the number 8. Do you have it on your brain? Think about its shape. Think of a snowman, the 8-ball on a pool table, a V-8 drink, etc. Eight is a beautiful number isn't it? Now try to forget it. Stop thinking about an 8; erase it from your mind; don't think of its shape, or the

> *Unless we have within us that which is above us, we will soon give in to the pressures around us.*

amount for which it stands. Repent of the number 8! You can't do it, can you? The more you try to forget the 8, the more it's there. The same is true of a sinful thought. The more you focus on repenting of it, the harder it is to put it off.

Try this: Think of the number 100. Add 4 to it; subtract 14 from it; divide it by 3; add 20; multiply it by 2; and then subtract 99. Did you think of that other number during that little sequence? You shouldn't have. (You should have the number 1 on your mind right now.) You will never rid your mind of sinful thoughts by focusing on how important it is to get rid of them. You must "replace" those thoughts. *"And the peace of God, which passeth all understanding, shall keep your hearts and minds through Christ Jesus. Finally, brethren, whatsoever things are true, whatsoever things are honest, whatsoever things are just, whatsoever things are pure, whatsoever things are lovely, whatsoever things are of good report; if there be any virtue, and if there be any praise, **think on these things**. Those things, which ye have both learned, and received, and heard, and seen in me, do: and the God of peace shall be with you"* [Emphasis mine] (Philippians 4:7–9).

Your mind is a lot like the desktop of your computer. Whatever you leave on that desktop will be staring you in the face every time you log on. But if you will take the time to click on those unwanted items and drag them over to your "recycle bin" or "trash can" you won't remember that they are on your computer. Now to be sure, they are still in your computer, and you can find them (or your server can) if you go digging in the trash can, but if they are "out of sight," they are "out of mind."

When we continually feed our minds the wrong data day after day, is it any wonder that we struggle with the same sinful thought patterns that lead us into sinful actions? Why don't you "click" on those wrong thoughts today and drag them under the blood of Christ? *"If we confess our sins, he is faithful and just to forgive us our sins, and to cleanse us from all unrighteousness"* (1 John 1:9). But don't stop there! Replace those wrong thoughts with right thoughts.

After confessing your sins first thing each morning, go ahead and put something on the desktop of your mind that will help you to think right and do right. Reading Scripture is a great start. Why not try memorizing a verse? Sing a hymn? Repeat a quote from last Sunday's sermon? Think about five people who have serious needs and pray for them. After a few of these disciplines to start your day, you won't be thinking about your "number 8" any more, and with time you'll forget about it altogether because your mind has been "renewed" through **Repentance, Resistance,** and **Replacement.**

Study Questions

1. What are we to do with our wickedness according to Acts 8:22?

2. List three or four sinful thought patterns that could threaten your life's direction.

3. What analogy does the Scripture use in Ephesians 5:18? Expound upon the truth found in this verse.

4. The replacement theory—putting off the sinful nature and putting on a Spirit-filled life—is found throughout the Bible. God emphasizes "replacement" in several places throughout Scripture. Read the following Scriptures and summarize each replacement that was made: Psalm 1:1–2, Ephesians 4:28, and Romans 12:9–21.

5. The old must be replaced by that which is new. Write out Colossians 3:8–10.

Memory Verse

"Not that we are sufficient of ourselves to think any thing as of ourselves; but our sufficiency is of God;"—2 Corinthians 3:5

CHAPTER TWELVE

Guided by a Christ-like Mind

W hen we get "our" thoughts out of the way, we can then develop the mind of Christ. *"But ye have not so learned Christ; If so be that the ye have heard him, and have been taught by him, as the truth is in Jesus"* (Ephesians 4:20–21). There used to be a popular phrase that seemed to be everywhere. It was "What would Jesus do?" Many abbreviated it to WWJD. I'm sure this served as a good reminder to people who would see it printed somewhere or engraved on a bracelet to think about their actions. But prior to that we need to ask WWJT! (What would Jesus Think?)

It would be remiss to write a book on the subject of our minds without studying the words of Paul to the Philippians in chapter two, *"Let this mind be in you, which was also in Christ Jesus: Who, being in the form of God, thought it not robbery to be equal with God: But made himself of no reputation, and took upon him the form of a servant, and was made in the likeness of men: And being found in fashion as a man, he humbled himself, and became obedient unto death, even the death of the cross"* (Philippians 2:5–8). What are the characteristics of a Christ-like mind?

A Mind of Selflessness

Jesus Christ is God! He always has been and always will be. He *"thought it not robbery to be equal with God"* because He is God. When Jesus Christ claimed to be God, many thought He was blasphemous and plotted to kill Him, but He was merely telling the truth. *"In the beginning was the Word, and the Word was with God, and the Word was God"* (John 1:1). But Jesus Christ, God in the flesh, *"made himself of no reputation"* (Philippians 2:7A). What a contrast to the "climb the ladder of success" syndrome that exists today. Man is constantly padding his resume and adding to his credentials. Young people cheat to achieve grades worthy of a scholarship. Adults lie about their past and do whatever it takes to appear smarter, younger (or older), and more experienced because after all "perception is reality."

Standing between us and eternal success is self! We are our own worst enemy. D. L. Moody said, "The man I fear the most is the one who walks underneath this hat." When Abraham Lincoln was running for president of the United States, a reporter asked him if he feared any of his opponents. Lincoln thought for a moment and responded, "Yes, one." The reporter was surprised since he was doing very well in the polls. He said, "Really, which one do you fear?" Lincoln said, "I fear a man named Lincoln. If I am defeated in this election, it will be by a man named Lincoln."

One day I was reading in 2 Timothy and came to chapter three. I read, *"This know also, that in the last days perilous times shall come"* (2 Timothy 3:1). I paused for a moment and thought: These must be the last days because they sure seem to be perilous. Who would have thought that we would be dealing with the problems of our society? Wars, political corruption, crime, gangs, immorality, etc.

are in the headlines on a daily basis. It seems that "evil men and seducers" are waxing worse and worse. But then I read in this verse, *"For men shall be lovers of their own selves"* (2 Timothy 3:2a). It was like the Holy Spirit took a dagger and plunged it into my chest. When God defines the last days, He does not speak of crime, or war, or same gender marriages. The last days will be characterized by selfishness!

Perhaps the greatest compliment ever given to the Lord Jesus Christ was given by Paul who said, *"For even Christ pleased not himself"* (Romans 15:3A). Not one single day of His eternal existence was ever lived for Himself, for He said, *"And he that sent me is with me: the Father hath not left me alone; I do always those things that please him"* (John 8:29). How much of the last twenty-four hours did we spend pleasing Him? The honest truth is, we are often characterized by, *"For all seek their own, not the things which are Jesus Christ's"* (Philippians 2:21).

No one is so empty as the man who is filled with thoughts of only himself. God sends no one away empty except for the people who are filled with themselves. Bob Zuppke, a famous football coach, once asked the question, "What makes a man fight?" He answered his own question by saying, "Two forces are at war in every fighter, the ego and the goal. An overdose of self-love, coddling of the ego, makes bums of men who ought to be champions. Forgetfulness of self, complete absorption in the goal often makes champions out of bums" (Charles L. Allen, *Joyful Living in the Fourth Dimension*, Baker Book House Company, 1983). Remember, our goal is to become like Christ. The Apostle Paul was absorbed with that goal, *"That I may know him, and the power of his resurrection, and the fellowship of his sufferings, being made conformable unto his death"* (Philippians 3:10).

> *"Who...worshipped and served the creature more than the Creator."*
> *—Romans 1:25*

A Mind of Service

" *...and took upon him the form of a servant, and was made in the likeness of men*" (Philippians 2:7B). "*For ye know the grace of our Lord Jesus Christ, that, though he was rich, yet for your sakes he became poor, that ye through his poverty might be rich*" (2 Corinthians 8:9). Jesus Christ, as God, left His throne in Heaven, wrapped Himself in flesh, and came to this sin-cursed world to serve! "*Even as the Son of man came not to be ministered unto, but to minister, and to give his life a ransom for many*" (Matthew 20:28).

My cousin, my sister, and I were playing outside one day when I was a small boy. The two of them were three years older than I was and were talking about what they wanted to be when they got big. Finally, they decided to ask me. They said, "Hey John, what do you want to be when you get big?" I wasn't very smart then (I'm still not). I responded, "I want to be a fire truck." Obviously at that young age, I didn't know the difference between a fire truck and a fireman. Later, they decided to get another laugh, and so they asked me again about my goal in life. I decided to change my answer since they embarrassed me the last time. I said, "I want to be a hospital." They laughed even louder as I apparently didn't know the difference between a hospital and a doctor.

Growing up there were many things I thought about doing. Once as a teenager I thought I wanted to be a barber, but that was back in the 1960s when no one was getting their hair cut. I decided that would be a dumb idea! Did you know that the greatest goal we could have for our lives is to be a servant? We are to have Christ's mind, and His mind was to serve. I tell our college students often that when they graduate, they ought to go out and find the lowest rung on the ladder. In a world where everyone is climbing the ladder of success, there won't be much competition for that bottom rung. Grab that place of lowly service and hang on, because one day God is going to turn the ladder around! "*For whosoever exalteth himself shall be abased; and he that humbleth himself shall be exalted*" (Luke 14:11).

Albert Einstein declared, "It is high time that the ideal of success should be replaced by the ideal of service." Too many people spell service, "serve us." Someone has said that the best exercise for our hearts is to bend down several times a day to help someone else. You say, "I don't have any talent or ability." God is not looking for ability; He's looking for availability, pliability, and dependability. The back porch light can do something the sun cannot—shine at night! God didn't save you to sit, soak, and sour. He saved you to stand, strive, and serve.

By the way, that's where the joy of the Christian life is found— in serving. The song writer wrote, "There is joy in serving Jesus." That is exactly what Jesus taught, *"If ye know these things, happy are ye if ye do them"* (John 13:17). Jesus didn't promise joy to those who simply *know* the Bible. He promises joy to those who *do* what they know. You can memorize all 31,000 verses in the Bible, but that won't make you happy. Karl Marx had Matthew, Mark, Luke, and John memorized as a teenager and could recite them perfectly in public, but he died an atheist.

Years ago I was preaching a revival meeting in a small town in Wyoming. One of the men in the church would faithfully preach in the nursing home across the street on Sunday afternoons. After the Sunday services, he thought, "Some of those people would enjoy these special services if I would bring them." Every night, he would arrive early, go across the street, and bring a number of those people over to the church in their wheelchairs.

On Tuesday night he brought a woman who did not appear to be extremely old, but was paralyzed from her waist down. He parked her in the center aisle about half-way back next to his family. She listened intently to the message and at the invitation time, looked up at the man who had brought her and said, "I want to go up there." He unlocked the brake on her chair and wheeled her forward. Upon arriving at the front, she told the pastor that she wanted to be saved, and several moments later was led to Christ by one of the women in the church.

She returned the next evening and on her way out, after shaking my hand, she said to the pastor, "Pastor, I got saved last night and now I know that I need to be baptized. Would you be able to baptize me?" He said, "Ma'am I would be delighted to baptize you. Here in our church we baptize on Sunday nights and if you could come this next Sunday night and give your testimony to one of our deacons, we could baptize you. Would that work out for you?" She said, "That would be great, but…." The pastor said, "Don't worry about a thing. I will get a couple of the deacons to help me and we will carry you down into the baptistery in your wheelchair. Then I will baptize you right in your chair. How does that sound?" She said, "Pastor, that would be wonderful!" Then she paused and said, "Pastor, after I get baptized and join the church, I want to work in the nursery." I thought to myself, "you've got to be kidding!" I mean, I know of people who ended up in wheelchairs *because of* working in the nursery, but she was already in one!

I guess the pastor must have had the same puzzled look on his face, because she pointed her finger up at him and said, "You don't think I'm too decrepit do you?" He said, "Oh no, not at all; we'll get you in there." Don't you love that spirit? No one would have thought any less of this woman if all she did was come to church, but God had done something in her life and now she wanted to serve Him. Do you have that mind to serve? It's the mind of Christ.

Now be careful, because if you tell God you're willing to serve Him, He will more than likely give you a chance to prove it. Here in our ministry, our pastor has taught us to greet people and say, "Is there anything that I can do for you?" It sounds great, is quite impressive, but becomes very routine. We say it to the UPS man who delivers packages, to first-time visitors in church, to prospective students, to anyone who dares step foot on our campus. We don't really mean it; we just say it!

A few years back, an elderly lady in our church had become ill and was hospitalized. Reports were coming back that she may not have long to live. I had met this couple years ago in a revival meeting here in California. The man had a great solo voice and used to sing in revival meetings where I would preach. They were a delightful couple and I was thrilled to catch up with them when I started preaching revival meetings at the Lancaster Baptist Church in 1986. When I assumed my position with the college, I was excited to see them more often and enjoyed their friendship and fellowship. Now she was perhaps on her deathbed and I knew that I needed to go up and see them. But good intentions got eaten up by "to do lists" and I kept putting it off. I knew that I would deeply regret not going up and having prayer with them if she should slip into eternity.

One day as I finished my last class around 1:00 PM, I decided that everything else was going to have to wait. I jumped in my car and headed for the hospital. Calling back to my office, I informed my secretary that I would be back on campus in an hour—I was headed to the hospital. Upon entering the room, I went over to the bedside and offered some words of encouragement, read some Scripture, and prayed. This wonderful servant of Christ for many years, smiled, thanked me and drifted back to sleep.

I sat down with her husband and we talked for about forty minutes about various things including the funeral that he wanted for his dear wife. I glanced at my watch—it was ten minutes until two. I said, "I need to be getting back to the office. Let me have a word of prayer with you." We bowed our heads and prayed and when I finished, I stood up and said, "I've got to be going; It was great to visit with you; I'll be praying for you; *Is there anything I can do for you?*"

He stood up and said, "Yes, there is!" I was stunned. No one had ever responded this way before. Pastor Chappell had not taught us—as far as I could remember—what to say next. So, I said, "What is it?" He exclaimed, "I want a pair of shoes just like Pastor Chappell's." I said, "You do?" He said, "Yup, and I know you can get 'em for me." I said, "You mean the loafers with the little tassels on the top." "Those are the ones," he said. "What color?" I asked. He said, "Black." I asked "What size?" He said, "Seven." Heading for the door, I called back, "I'll be back in an hour."

I had a smile on my face and a spring in my step *until* I got to the hallway. Suddenly the smile and the spring was gone. My pace quickened to a frantic jog as I headed for the stairs and out to my car. "A pair of shoes! Lord, what's this all about? I don't have time to buy a pair of shoes! Do I look like a shopper? I scanned my brain for the nearest store that might have a pair of shoes. There was a Marshall's store about a mile away. I raced to the store praying that God would let me find them quickly. Marshalls didn't have them. I headed to Mervyns a few blocks further down the street. No luck. I was learning now that size seven was a very small size for a man's shoe! Both of these stores had informed me that they did not carry any men's shoes in a size seven, much less the kind I was looking for.

I thought, I'm going to have to go to the mall! I hate the mall! Making my way down the freeway, I pulled into the parking lot and ran to the first "normal" store—J.C. Penny. Then to Sears, then to Gottschalks—I was working my way up. Finally, there was only one store left: Dillards! Second cousin to Macys. I never shop there except during the January sale. They had them! Just like Pastor Chappell's; in black; and size seven. I picked them up and turned them over to see the price: $129.95!

I didn't have that kind of cash on me, but I did possess a credit card and so bought the shoes.

About an hour after I had left, I walked back into that hospital room with a box of shoes. I said, "There you go—just like Pastor Chappell's." He said, "Thank you." I said, "You're welcome" and walked out. You know, I've never seen that man wear those shoes! Oh, I look every time I see him. As I shake his hand, I'm pulling up his trousers with the other hand. To this day I have no idea why he wanted those shoes, but I know why God had me go and get them. God taught me an important lesson that day about serving. It's one thing to sing the songs about serving and talk the talk. It's quite another matter to walk the walk! It took me a while to pay off the price of those shoes, but it was a joy to do so because God had given me a chance to serve!

A Mind of Submission

"And being found in fashion as a man, he humbled himself, and became obedient unto death, even the death of the cross" (Philippians 2:8). From a very early age, man seems to think that the ideal is to be autonomous rather than submissive. But the mind of Christ is to submit.

"...My meat is to do the will of him that sent me, and to finish his work" (John 4:34). *"He went away again the second time, and prayed, saying, O my Father, if this cup may not pass away from me, except I drink it, thy will be done"* (Matthew 26:42).

Are you willing to do anything that God asks you to do? Is there anything that you are unwilling to do?

Soon after we were married, my wife Diane and I joined a Baptist church that was growing and exciting. While we were on the road in evangelism most weeks during the year, we always enjoyed coming home to our church and being as much a part as we could. The pastor and his family became dear friends as did many of the couples in that church. But trouble came. Soon we were losing people, and all kinds of rumors began to circulate—none of which turned out to be true. I was restless. As an evangelist, I could choose to live wherever I wanted. I wanted to be a part of a strong church, and I was tempted to leave that struggling situation.

On a particular Wednesday night during the song service, we were singing the song, "I'll go where you want me to go, dear Lord." After the first verse, our pastor who had founded that church and had faithfully served for nearly twenty-five years, interrupted the song leader and said, "When we get to the chorus on this next verse, let's sing, 'I'll stay where you want me to stay, dear Lord.'" The Holy Spirit struck the dagger to my heart once again that night. It would have been easy to "go" anywhere, but there at that moment, the Holy Spirit wanted me to submit and "stay." You don't soon forget those lessons.

Our critics often say that as Christians we are under some kind of "mind control." I plead guilty. Paul said, "...*we have the mind of Christ*" (1 Corinthians 2:16b). Wouldn't you much rather have the mind of Christ than the mind of the flesh or the mind of the world? "*For they that are after the flesh do mind the things of the flesh; but they that are after the Spirit the things of the Spirit. For to be carnally minded is death; but to be spiritually minded is life and peace*" (Romans 8:5–6). "*Forasmuch then as Christ hath suffered for us in the flesh, arm yourselves likewise with the same mind: for he that hath suffered in the flesh hath ceased from sin; That he no longer should live the rest of his time in the flesh to the lusts of men, but to the will of God*" (1 Peter 4:1–2).

> *The purpose in life is not to find your freedom, but your Master.*
> —*P.T. Forsyth*

How will you choose to live the rest of your time? In the lust of your flesh or with the mind of Christ?

Years ago, I was privileged to speak at a summer camp for teenagers with Dr. Ed. Nelson, long time pastor and educator. In one of his messages, he told how he and his wife were walking down the street to a restaurant in Denver, Colorado one day when they spotted the headline of the newspaper in a vending machine. The headline read: **LUCY DIES!** Dr. Nelson looked at his wife and said,

"Who's Lucy?" She didn't know either and so upon sitting down to eat they asked the waitress who Lucy was. She said Lucille Ball from "I Love Lucy." Dr. Nelson and his wife looked at each other and shrugged. Neither of them had ever heard of Lucille Ball or the famous television program.

I thought to myself, "that's impossible," everybody in that era had heard of "I Love Lucy." But not the Nelsons. He went on to explain that he and his wife had never watched a single moment of television in their entire lives up to that point. I was stunned! Not even the news? The World Series? The Super Bowl? Nothing?

As I contemplated that later, I thought, "What have they missed?" The answer—not much! Their minds and hearts were not cluttered with non-essential things. (Not to mention the countless temptations to sin that they were never exposed to either.) Their lifetime of ministry was testimony to their minds being filled with the things that are true, honest, just, pure, lovely, of good report, virtuous, and praise-worthy. We have the same choice.

Study Questions

1. God wants us to have a selfless mind. However, when you read Romans 1:25, does this verse describe your Christianity? Explain your answer.

2. The greatest goal we could have for our lives is to be a servant. We are to have Christ's mind, and His mind is to serve. How can you serve God's people this week? In what ways can you serve more this week than you did last week?

3. Are you willing to do anything that God asks you to do? Is there anything that you are unwilling to do?

4. P. T. Forsyth said, "The purpose in life is not to find your freedom, but your Master." Give five reasons that show how you are living a life that is directed to becoming more like your Master. (Example: (1) I memorize Scripture to have the mind of Christ.)

5. When we get "our thoughts" out of the way, we can then develop the mind of Christ. Write out Ephesians 4:20–21.

Memory Verse

"Let this mind be in you, which was also in Christ Jesus: Who, being in the form of God, thought it not robbery to be equal with God: But made himself of no reputation, and took upon him the form of a servant, and was made in the likeness of men: And being found in fashion as a man, he humbled himself, and became obedient unto death, even the death of the cross."—Philippians 2:5–8

Conclusion

An *autistic savant* (historically described as *idiot savant*) is a person with both autism and savant syndrome. Savant syndrome describes a person having a severe developmental or mental handicap with extraordinary mental abilities not found in most people. This means a lower than average general intelligence (IQ) but very high narrow intelligence in one or more fields. Savant syndrome skills involve striking feats of memory and arithmetic calculation and sometimes include unusual abilities in art or music. Savant syndrome is sometimes abbreviated as "savantism," and individuals with the syndrome are often nicknamed *savants* (Wikipedia, http://en.wikipedia.org/wiki/Autistic_savant).

Most autistic savants have extensive mental abilities called *splinter skills*. However, it is important to notice that people with a high general intelligence can demonstrate the same skills; savant disabilities are not necessary for these skills. They can recall facts, numbers, license plates, maps, and extensive lists of sports and weather statistics after only being exposed to them once. Some savants can mentally note and then recall perfectly a very long sequence of music, numbers, or speech. Some, dubbed mental calculators, can do exceptionally fast arithmetic, including prime factorization. Other skills include precisely estimating distances and angles by sight, calculating the day of the week for any given date over the span of tens of thousands of years, and being able to accurately gauge the passing of time without a clock. Most autistic savants have a single special skill while others have multiple skills. Usually these abilities are concrete, non-symbolic, right hemisphere skills as opposed to left hemisphere skills that tend to be more sequential, logical, and symbolic (Ibid.).

Savants are a fascination to me. If you want something that will literally stun you, do a "Google" search on the subject of "savants." Type in names such as Kim Peek (He has become very popular after being the basis for the fictional film "Rain Man" produced in 1988. Peek can read two pages at a time—one with each eye—in eight seconds and has a 98% retention!), Daniel Tammet (Tammet, who has been called the "Brain Man," found and then memorized the endless numbers embodied in the Greek letter "Pi." Normally "Pi" is rounded off to 3.14, but the number actually goes on into infinity. After finding the sequence of these numbers, Tammet over several weeks memorized 22,514 digits in order and then went to Oxford University in England and in just over five hours, with several university students checking the lists, recited all 22,514 numbers in sequence without a single mistake!), or Stephen Wiltshire (known as the "Human Camera," took a 45 minute helicopter ride over Rome and then over the next three days drew an exact replica of every building and street in the city on a five and a half yard canvass from memory!).

Scientists have been studying these people for years (there are only around fifty known savants in the world today), and have yet to discover what "unlocks" their brain to these incredible abilities in certain areas. For years it has been believed that humans only use about ten percent of their brains. (Some of us have trouble remembering our four digit code at the ATM!) Man can only speculate about the potential of the human brain.

In my brief research on savants, I noticed that in many of them, it seems that there was a certain catastrophic event which seemed to "unlock" this portion of their brain. In the case of Daniel Tammet, his mother noticed a change after an epileptic seizure. Man was created in God's image, after His likeness, right? *"And God said, Let us make man in our image, after our likeness"* (Genesis 1:26a). Imagine the capability of Adam's brain—made after the image of God! No wonder he had no problem naming the animals and caring for the entire creation.

But a catastrophic event took place in the garden one day. Man disobeyed God and when he did, he was immediately separated from God. His body (and mind) were now tainted with sin and he would never be the same. God's perfect creation had been marred by sin. When Adam sinned, the entire human race that followed him was now flawed as well. *"Wherefore, as by one man sin entered into the world, and death by sin; and so death passed upon all men, for that all have sinned"* (Romans 5:12). Notice how Paul describes the effects of sin on our lives, *"Wherein in time past ye walked according to the course of this world, according to the prince of the power of the air, the spirit that now worketh in the children of disobedience: Among whom also we all had our conversation in times past in the lusts of our flesh, fulfilling the desires of the flesh **and of the mind;** and were by nature the children of wrath, even as others"* [Emphasis mine] (Ephesians 2:2–3).

Could it be that all of our minds possess stunning capabilities, such as these savants demonstrate in single areas, but because of sin these areas of our brains remain "locked"? Only God knows. But I know this: another catastrophic-like event is going to take place!

"Behold, I shew you a mystery; We shall not all sleep, but we shall all be changed, In a moment, in the twinkling of an eye, at the last trump: for the trumpet shall sound, and the dead shall be raised incorruptible, and we shall be changed. For this corruptible must put on incorruption, and this mortal must put on immortality. So when this corruptible shall have put on incorruption, and this mortal shall have put on immortality, then shall be brought to pass the saying that is written, Death is swallowed up in victory. O death, where is thy sting? O grave, where is thy victory? The sting of death is sin; and the strength of sin is the law. But thanks be to God, which giveth us the victory through our Lord Jesus Christ."—1 CORINTHIANS 15:51–57

When Jesus Christ comes, we are going to be changed! We will have new bodies to be sure, but we will also have new minds. The capabilities that God created us with will be restored! *"Beloved, now are we the sons of God, and it doth not yet appear what we shall be: but we know that, when he shall appear, we shall be like him; for we shall see him as he is"* (1 John 3:2).

But while we are stuck here with sin-flawed bodies and minds, don't neglect to read the next verse, *"And every man that hath this hope in him purifieth himself, even as he is pure"* (1 John 3:3). Ask God right now to help you get started.

Ask Him to give you a **"Brain Wash."**

Ask Him to help you keep the **"Brain Door Closed."**

Ask Him to enable you to be under His **"Mind Control."**

You'll be more of the person God wants you to be because *"...as he thinketh in his heart, so is he"* (Proverbs 23:7A).

The Putting Off–Putting On Principle

P aul tells us in 2 Timothy 3:16, that *"All scripture is given by inspiration of God, and is profitable for…"*

*Doctrine: That's what's **right.***
*Reproof: That's what's **wrong.***
*Correction: That's **how to get right.***
*Instruction in righteousness: That's **how to stay right.***

The truth is, most of us know when things are wrong in our lives. God's Word has been *"…written in their hearts, their conscience also bearing witness…"* (Romans 2:15). The preaching of God's Word or the reading of it exposes the errors in our lives and causes us to change our minds about our sin and repent.

However, we must go a step further, because the Bible does. If all we do is empty our lives of sin, we leave a void for the devil to fill with something else. *"When the unclean spirit is gone out of a man, he walketh through dry places, seeking rest, and findeth none. Then he saith, I will return into my house from when I came out; and when he is come, he findeth it empty, swept, and garnished. Then goeth he, and taketh with himself seven other spirits more wicked than himself, and they enter in and dwell there: and the last state of that man is worse than the first. Even so shall it be also unto this wicked generation*" (Matthew 12:43–45).

The "old" must be replaced with "new" or it will be replaced by worse "old." Notice carefully this principle in Paul's instruction in Ephesians 4:

> "*But ye have not so learned Christ; If so be that ye have heard him, and have been taught by him, as the truth is in Jesus: That ye* **put off** *concerning the former conversation the old man, which is corrupt according to the deceitful lusts; And be renewed in the spirit of your mind; And that ye* **put on** *the new man, which after God is created in righteousness and true holiness. Wherefore* **putting away** *lying, speak every man truth with his neighbour: for we are members one of another. Be ye angry, and sin not: let not the sun go down upon your wrath: Neither give place to the devil. Let him that stole steal no more: but rather let him labour, working with his hands the thing which is good, that he may have to give to him that needeth. Let no corrupt communication proceed out of your mouth, but that which is good to the use of edifying, that it may minister grace unto the hearers. And grieve not the holy Spirit of God, whereby ye are sealed unto the day of redemption. Let all bitterness, and wrath, and anger, and clamour, and evil speaking, be* **put away** *from you with all malice: And be ye kind one to another, tenderhearted, forgiving one another, even as God for Christ's sake hath forgiven you.*"
> [Emphasis mine]—EPHESIANS 4:20–32

"Put off" and "Put on." As Paul deals with certain sins, he not only instructs the believers to put them off, but then specifically states what should be put in their place. For Christian growth and maturity to take place the old habits of sin must be broken, and new patterns of thinking and living must replace them.

Someone has said, "You can't teach an old dog new tricks." Well, first of all we are not talking about "dogs." We are talking about "people." Second, we are not talking about "tricks." We are talking about "holy living by the grace of God." Either we believe the Bible or we don't! God is in the business of "changing lives." He changes us at conversion and makes us brand new creatures (2 Corinthians 5:17), and then changes us continually through the process of sanctification (2 Corinthians 3:18). *"There hath no temptation taken you but such as is common to man: but God is faithful, who will not suffer you to be tempted above that ye are able; but will with the temptation also make a way to escape, that ye may be able to bear it"* (1 Corinthians 10:13).

The Bible is filled with "instead of's." For example, in James 5:12 it says, *"But above all things, my brethren, swear not, neither by heaven, neither by the earth, neither by any other oath: **but** let your yea be yea; and your nay, nay; lest ye fall into condemnation."* What about Psalm 1:1–2? *"Blessed is the man that walketh not in the counsel of the ungodly, nor standeth in the way of sinners, nor sitteth in the seat of the scornful. **But** his delight is in the law of the Lord; and in his law doth he meditate day and night."* The wrong sin, the wrong habit, is replaced by the right action, the right habit!

Listen to James, *"Submit yourselves therefore to God. Resist the devil, and he will flee from you. Draw nigh to God, and he will draw nigh to you. Cleanse your hands, ye sinners; and purify your hearts, ye double minded. Be afflicted, and mourn, and weep: let your laughter be turned to mourning, and your joy to heaviness. Humble yourselves in the sight of the Lord, and he shall lift you up"* (James 4:7–10). Or what about Ephesians 5:18? *"And be not drunk with wine, wherein is excess; but be filled with the Spirit."*

There is no such thing as "instant holiness." *"Enoch walked with God"* (Genesis 5:24). *"So Jotham became mighty, because he **prepared his ways** before the LORD his God"* [Emphasis mine] (2 Chronicles 27:6). Paul instructed Timothy to *"**exercise** thyself rather unto godliness"* [Emphasis mine] (1 Timothy 4:7). Spiritual maturity is an ongoing process of replacing the old with the new. Enoch didn't get from point A to point B in one step. He *walked* with God. *"...If any man will come after me, let him deny himself, and take up his cross **daily**, and follow me"* [Emphasis mine] (Luke 9:23).

God **exposes** the old and **explains** the new. He teaches **repentance** but also **replacement**. He commands us to **deny** the old and **dedicate** to the new; **forsake sin** and **follow the Saviour; starve** the flesh and **saturate** ourselves with the Spirit. If we are going to be healthy sheep, we must have a balanced diet.

I have listed eighty-two common sins that need to be "put off" from our lives and their counterparts that should be "put on" in their places. With each of these "old" and "new" habits, we have listed several verses that reinforce the principle. When you are struggling with an area in your life, memorize these verses that rebuke the wrong and reinforce the right. Jesus confronted the temptations of Satan with Scripture and we are wise to take the "sword of the Spirit, which is the Word of God" and do likewise.

"Put Off"	"Put On"
1. Lack of Love *1 Thess. 3:12; 1 John 4:7–8, 20*	1. Love *John 15:12; John 13:35;* *1 Peter 1:22*
2. Judging *1 Cor. 4:5; Rom. 14:4; James 4:12;* *Matthew 7:1–5*	2. Search my own sin *John 8:9; John 15:22;* *Psalm 139:23–24;* *Jer. 17:10*

3. Bitterness
James 3:14–15; Eph. 4:31;
Heb. 12:15

3. Tenderheartedness
Col. 3:12; Rom. 12:10;
2 Peter 1:5–7

4. Unforgiving spirit
Matt. 6:14; Mark 11:25–26

4. Forgiving spirit
Matt. 6:14; Luke 17:4;
Col. 3:13

5. Pride
Prov. 11:2; Prov. 21:4; Prov. 28:25;
Prov. 16:18

5. Humility
James 4:6; Prov. 16:19;
Prov. 22:4; Prov. 29:23;
Matt. 18:4

6. Selfishness
Isaiah 5:8; Matt. 25:43; Phil. 2:21

6. Death to self
John 12:24; Matt. 16:25;
1 Cor. 10:24; Phil. 2:4;
Gal. 2:20

7. Boasting (conceit)
Gal. 6:3; Prov. 17:19; Prov. 25:6–7
1 Cor. 4:7

7. Humility
Prov. 27:2; Matt. 23:12;
1 Pet. 5:5–6

8. Stubbornness
2 Chron. 24:19; Acts 7:51;
1 Sam. 15:23

8. Submission
Rom. 6:13; Matt. 6:10;
Matt. 26:39

9. Lack of Submission
2 Peter 2:10; Eph. 6:6; 2 Tim. 3:6

9. Broken will
Matt. 6:10; Psalm 40:8;
Matt. 12:50

10. Rebellion
Jer. 44:16; Zech. 7:11;
1 Sam. 15:23

10. Submission
Joel 2:12–13; Luke 1:38;
James 4:7

11. Disobedience
Eph. 5:6; 2 Thess. 1:8; Heb. 2:2–3

11. Obedience
Heb. 5:9; Deut. 26:16;
1 Sam. 15:22; Acts 5:29

12. Ungratefulness
    Luke 17:17–18; Deut. 32:6:
    Rom. 1:21

12. Thankfulness
    Eph. 5:20; Deut. 8:10;
    Psalm 100:4; Col. 3:15

13. Impatience
    Ecc. 7:8; Psalm 40:1; James 1:2–4

13. Patience
    Luke 21:19; Rom. 12:12;
    Heb. 10:36; James 1:4;
    James 5:7

14. Discontent
    Prov. 15:16; Deut. 32:32;
    Phil. 4:11–12

14. Satisfaction
    Heb. 13:5; 1 Tim. 6:6

15. Covetousness
    Jer. 6:13; Hab. 2:9; Luke 12:15;
    Exodus 20:17

15. Yielded rights
    Col. 3:5; Rom. 13:14;
    Gal. 5:16

16. Murmur
    John 6:43; Phil. 2:14; Prov. 19:3

16. Gratefulness
    1 Cor. 10:10; 1 Thess 5:18

17. Complaining
    Psalm 77:3; Jude 15–16

17. Contentment
    Heb. 13:5; Psalm 142:4

18. Sassing
    Isaiah 57:4; John 6:43

18. Respect for authority
    Eph. 5:21; Heb. 13:17;
    1 Cor. 16:16

19. Irritation to others
    Prov. 17:14; Prov. 26:17;
    Prov. 25:8

19. Preferring in love
    Phil. 2:3–4; 2 Tim. 2:14

20. Jealousy
    Gen. 37:4; Prov. 27:4

20. Trust
    1 Cor. 13:4; Prov. 3:5–6

21. Strife
    Prov. 3:30; Prov. 20:3; James 3:16

21. Esteem others
    Luke 6:31; Mark 12:31;
    Rom. 13:10; Rom. 15:1–2;
    Gal. 5:14

22. Losing temper
Prov. 14:17; Prov. 16:32

22. Self control
Rom. 5:3–4; Prov. 19:11

23. Bodily harm
Acts 16:28; Prov. 16:29

23. Gentleness
1 Thess. 2:7; 2 Tim. 2:4;
James 3:17

24. Anger
Ecc. 7:9; Prov. 14:17

24. Self control
Gal. 5:24–25; 1 Cor. 9:25

25. Wrath
Psalm 37:8; James 1:19–20

25. Self control
Gal. 5:24–25; Rom. 6:12

26. Hatred
Matt. 5:21–22

26. Kindness
1 Cor. 13:3; Matt. 22:39

27. Murder
Matt. 19:18; Rom. 13:9; Ex. 20:13

27. Love
Rom. 13:10; 1 Peter 1:22

28. Gossip
Titus 3:2; James 3:6; James 4:11

28. Speak with praise
Rom. 14:19; Eph. 4:12;
Eph. 4:29

29. Lying
Prov. 12:19; Psalm 5:6;
Psalm 101:7; Prov. 12:22; Col. 3:9

29. Speaking truth
Zech. 8:16; Eph. 6:14

30. Bad language
Eph. 4:31; Eph. 4:29

30. Edify
1 Tim. 4:12; Prov. 16:14;
Col. 4:6

31. Profanity
Ecc. 10:12; Psalm 109:17

31. Edify
1 Tim. 4:12; Prov. 25:11

32. Idle words
1 Tim. 6:3–4; Matt. 12:36

32. Bridled tongue
Prov. 21:23; James 3:2–3

33. Evil thoughts
1 Chron. 28:9; Prov. 15:26;
Prov. 23:7

33. Good thoughts
Phil. 4:8; Rom. 8:6;
Phil. 2:5

34. Bad motives
Prov. 6:18; Rom. 1:21;
Psalm 38:12; Gen. 11:6

34. Meditation
Psalm 19:14; Psalm 119:59;
Prov. 12:5

35. Complacency
Rev. 3:15; James 4:17

35. Diligence
Col. 3:23; Deut. 6:5;
Psalm 119:2; Jer. 29:13;
Ecc. 9:10

36. Hypocrisy
Matt. 23:23–25; Isaiah 29:13;
Job 8:13

36. Honesty
Eph. 4:25; Luke 6:46;
Rom. 2:21; James 3:10

37. Other gods
Josh. 24:14–15; Deut. 11:16

37. Christ in first place
Eph. 4:6; Matt. 6:33;
Acts 3:26

38. Loss of first love
Hosea 10:2; Matt. 24:12; Rev. 2:4

38. Meditate on Christ's love
1 John 4:10, 19

39. Lack of rejoicing
Psalm 85:6; Phil. 4:4

39. Rejoicing
1 Thess. 5:16; 1 Peter 1:8

40. Worry
Matt. 6:25–34

40. Trust
1 Peter 5:7; Phil. 4:6

41. Doubt
Luke 18:8; 1 John 5:4;
1 Thess. 5:24

41. Faith
Heb. 11:1; Luke 17:5

42. Unfaithfulness
Prov. 20:6; Prov. 25:19; 1 Cor. 4:2

42. Faithfulness
Psalm 31:23; Rev. 2:10;
Luke 19:17

43. Copping out
   Prov. 24:10; Matt. 24:26

43. Discipline
   Luke 14:27; 1 Cor. 9:24–27

44. Neglect of Bible study
   Psalm 119:9–11; 2 Tim. 3:14–17

44. Devotions
   Josh. 1:8; Isaiah 34:16;
   1 Tim. 2:15

45. Neglect of prayer
   Luke 18:1; Eph. 6:18;
   1 Chron. 16:11

45. Prayer
   Psalm 55:17; Heb. 4:16;
   Mark 1:35; 2 Chron. 7:14

46. No soulwinning
   Ezekiel 33:8–9

46. Soulwinning
   Prov. 11:30; Dan. 12:3;
   James 5:20; Matt. 4:19;
   Jude 22–23

47. Burying talents
   Matt. 25:14–30

47. Perfecting abilities
   Luke 12:48; 1 Cor. 4:2

48. Irresponsibility
   Prov. 24:30–34

48. Responsibility
   Eph. 4:1; Prov. 6:6–11

49. Procrastination
   James 4:13–15; Prov. 27:1

49. Discipline
   John 9:4; Psalm 95:7–8

50. Laziness
   Prov. 13:4; Prov. 20:4; Prov. 21:25;
   Eph. 5:15–16

50. Diligence
   1 Cor. 10:31; Prov. 22:29;
   2 Peter 3:14

51. Not doing your best
   Prov. 14:23; Ecc. 9:10

51. Doing your best
   Col. 3:23; 1 Cor. 14:12

52. Misconduct in church
   1 Tim. 3:15; Psalm 122:1

52. Reverence
   Ecc. 5:1; Psalm 26:8;
   Psalm 27:4

53. No tithing
   Mal. 3:7–10;

53. Tithing
   2 Cor. 9:6–7; 1 Cor. 16:1–2

54. Inhospitable
    1 Peter 4:9

54. Hospitality
    Rom. 12:13; Heb. 13:2

55. Temporal values
    Phil. 3:8; Hag. 1:5–7; Prov. 13:7;
    Matt. 6:19–21

55. Eternal values
    2 Tim. 2:4; Col. 3:2;
    1 Tim. 6:19

56. Following the crowd
    Prov. 29:25–26; I Cor. 15:33;
    Psalm 1:1; Prov. 4:14; Ex. 34:12

56. Following Christ
    Matt. 6:33; Isaiah 55:6;
    Acts 17:27

57. Cheating
    1 Peter 2:12; Prov. 15:3

57. Honesty
    Luke 8:15; Rom. 12:17

58. Stealing
    Ex. 20:15; 1 Peter 4:15; Eph. 4:28

58. Giving
    Luke 6:38; Prov. 3:9–10

59. Lack of moderation
    Col 3:13; Phil. 4:5

59. Balance
    2 Peter 1:5–10

60. Over-eating
    Prov. 23:21; Prov. 23:1–2

60. Self control
    1 Cor. 9:27; Luke 21:34;
    Luke 12:22

61. Speeding
    1 Peter 2:13–14

61. Obedience to civil law
    Ecc. 8:2; Rom. 13:1

62. Improper dating relationships
    Gen. 39:9; 1 Cor. 15:33

62. God's standards
    Phil. 1:20; 1 Cor. 6:19–20

63. Dating the wrong people
    2 Cor. 6:14

63. Equal yoke
    1 Cor. 6:12; Amos 3:3

64. Lust of the flesh
    Gal. 5:24; Rom. 6:6; 1 John 2:16

64. Pure desires
    1 Peter 2:11; Rom. 13:14;
    Col. 3:5

65. Lust of the eyes
Psalm 101:3; 1 John 2:16

65. Pure thoughts
Phil. 2:4; 1 Tim. 5:22

66. Fornication
1 Thess. 4:3–8

66. Purity
1 Cor. 10:8; Matt. 5:8;
Psalm 24:3–4

67. Necking / Petting
Prov. 5:20; 1 Cor. 7:1

67. Abstinence
1 Thess. 4:4; Heb. 13:4

68. Immodest dress
Prov. 11:22

68. Modesty
1 Tim. 2:9

69. Adultery
Matt. 5:27–28

69. Fidelity
Ex. 20:14; Prov. 5:18

70. Homosexuality
Rom. 1:26–27

70. God's purpose
1 Tim. 5:22; Gen. 2:24

71. Worldly hair styles
Phil. 1:27

71. Glorify God
1 Cor. 11:14–15

72. Worldly music
Psalm 95:1; 1 Cor. 14:15;
Prov. 23:7

72. Edifying music
Eph. 5:19; Col. 3:16

73. Dancing
1 Thess. 5:22

73. Glorify God
1 Cor. 10:31

74. Drugs
Rev. 21:8

74. God's Temple
1 Cor. 3:16–17

75. Drinking
Prov. 20:1; Isaiah 5:11;
Rom. 13:13; Prov. 23:20

75. God's Temple
Prov. 23:29–35

76. Smoking
1 Cor. 6:19–20

76. God's Temple
1 Cor. 3:16–17

77. Witchcraft / Astrology
    Deut. 18:10–11

78. Gambling
    Luke 15:13

79. Movies
    Matt. 6:22–23; Prov. 23:7

80. Stumbling block to others
    1 Cor. 8:9–12

81. Preferential treatment
    James 2:1–6

82. Presumption of the future
    James 4:13–14

77. One true God
    Micah 5:12–15

78. Stewardship
    1 Cor. 4:2

79. Example
    Psalm 101:3

80. Stepping stone
    Rom. 14:21; Rom. 15:1

81. Fairness
    Luke 6:31; 1 Tim. 5:21

82. Patience
    Prov. 27:1

How to Memorize Scripture

Often people come up to me after I preach and say, "My, you have a wonderful memory. I wish I could memorize like that! God has really gifted you with a great mind." I want to cry! Now don't misunderstand. I am what I am by the grace of God (1 Corinthians 15:10)! Paul said, *"For who maketh thee to differ from another? and what hast thou that thou didst not receive? now if thou didst receive it, why dost thou glory, as if thou hadst not received it?"* (1 Corinthians 4:7).

Usually, I respond to those comments with, "Well, I have a photographic mind, but I ran out of film a couple of years ago." They laugh, and that's the end of the conversation. But before you read any further, let me share with you the real secret to memorizing Scripture—"time and work." Now don't stop reading, because I think in the next few minutes, I can make that "time" effective and the "work" enjoyable.

Let me tell you first how it all started with me. When I was in college, I decided after an enjoyable freshman speech class to minor in the subject. I did it because I thought it would be fun, not because I thought I would ever use anything I was about to learn. Because of that minor in speech, I was required to participate in the college dramas that were performed on campus twice each year, as well as recite poetry and monologues in various services. I was also required to be in a recital at the end of my senior year. This called for a lot of memorizing. I was in the plays "As You Like It," "Hamlet," "The Robe," "Julius Caesar," and my favorite—"Cyrano!" My German nose helped me land that part! In "Cyrano" alone, I had over 1500 lines to memorize, and I also had to know "when" to say them, so I had to memorize the lines just before mine too! For my recital, I did the comedy, "Teahouse of the August Moon." I loved it and would do it all again if I had the chance.

But by the time graduation rolled around, my brain was fried! It couldn't hold any more "memory," and so for the next four years, I did not conscientiously memorize anything! But, I was always convicted that I should. I would listen to preachers quote portions of Scripture and think, I could do that. I was busy in revival work: writing sermons, preaching, winning souls, helping churches, being a husband and dad, etc., and so excused myself from any further discipline in the "study" area. But the Holy Spirit kept reminding me, "If you could memorize Shakespeare—you could memorize Scripture."

In October of 1978, we were holding a Christian school revival in Coleman, Wisconsin. I preached several times during the school day to various age groups, but there were no services or activities in the evening. The town of Coleman at that time had a population of three hundred and when five o'clock in the evening rolled around, the town shut down. Stores were not open, people disappeared from the streets, and everything became extremely quiet. I was bored to tears! My wife and I were traveling in a twenty-five-foot trailer.

Our oldest son John, was just a little over a year old. The first night after supper, I went to the gym and shot some baskets for a couple of hours, but there's only so much fun you can have by yourself. Finally, after a couple of nights of this, I announced to Diane that I was going inside the school to memorize some Bible verses.

The only reason I did it was because I was bored and needed something to kill time. As I sat there that first night contemplating where to start, I realized that almost every week in revivals, I would preach a message on the subject of Hell. So, that's where I started. In the next couple of hours, I had memorized about ten verses on Hell and was pretty proud of myself. It was kind of fun to "preach" them as I would memorize them in the big gym that would make my voice sound more powerful than it was. I got so excited about it that the next night I went back inside and went at it again. By the end of that week, I had memorized about thirty verses on Hell, including the entire passage in Luke sixteen about the rich man and Lazarus.

I really didn't plan for it to go any further than that. I had killed some time with something profitable and knew that I would probably not have too many weeks when I would ever be that bored again. Our next revival was in Hadley, Michigan and when we arrived, the pastor informed me that Monday evening would be Awana Parent's Night and that several unsaved couples would be there to watch a short program and then I would preach. I was excited about the opportunity to preach to a good number of lost people (there were eighteen visiting couples there that night), and decided to preach on "Hell." But for the first time in my life, instead of reading the verses from the Bible in my message, I quoted them. I can't explain the power and life I felt in those words, which were not mine, but God's! For the first time in my ministry I felt like I was preaching "the Word."

I believe there were twelve adults who trusted Christ in that service! The next morning, I was up at 4:00 AM memorizing verses, and I've been hooked on the power of God's Word ever since. But long before I ever discovered this potential, God wrote, *"And these words, which I command thee this day, shall be **in thine heart"*** [Emphasis mine] (Deuteronomy 6:6). *"Therefore shall ye lay up these my words **in your heart and in your soul…"*** [Emphasis mine] (Deuteronomy 11:18). *"Thy word have I hid **in my heart**, that I might not sin against thee"* [Emphasis mine] (Psalm 119:11). *"But what saith it? The word is nigh thee, even in thy mouth, and **in thy heart**: that is, the word of faith, which we preach"* [Emphasis mine] (Romans 10:8). *"Let the word of Christ **dwell in you** richly…"* [Emphasis mine] (Colossians 3:16).

Regardless of what this world teaches about success, God makes it clear that success only comes from one source, *"This book of the law shall not depart out of thy mouth; but thou shalt meditate therein day and night, that thou mayest observe to do according to all that is written therein: for then thou shalt make thy way prosperous, and then thou shalt have good **success"*** [Emphasis mine] (Joshua 1:8). This is the only time you will find the word "success" in the Bible and God states that it comes as a result of "meditating" on His Word. You can't meditate on something you haven't put in your heart!

There are many good "plans" out there to help you memorize, but let me share with you what has worked for me. It's a little bit unique, but remember, "time and work" are the key. The biblical principle is "what you sow is what you reap" so you'll get out of this in exact proportion to the time and energy you put in to it.

Choose a Specific Time And a Quiet Place

Very little gets accomplished in our lives that isn't planned. If you are seriously going to memorize Scripture, you must be willing to block off a section of time when you are free from other distractions of life. I'm not talking about your commute drive here or time in the check-out line at Wal Mart! I'm talking about time like Jesus spent alone in communion with His Father, *"And in the morning, rising up a great while before day, he went out, and departed into a solitary place, and there prayed"* (Mark 1:35). *"And when he had sent the multitudes away, he went up into a mountain apart to pray: and when the evening was come, he was there alone"* (Matthew 14:23).

Most of us today resist being "alone." We feel like we always have to be in the middle of the action. May I say that some of the loneliest people in the world are in the middle of a crowd. They are surrounded by people, but are lonely. There is a huge difference between loneliness and solitude. Solitude is something you choose, and you'd better, if you plan to survive in this world. We need time with God and His Word "alone"!

You say, "You don't understand my world. I'm surrounded by people from the time I get up until I go to bed. My time is never my own." And I say, that's why you're frustrated and about to "burn out!" In Mark chapter one, Jesus was surrounded by people (read his schedule beginning in verse twenty one!) But the next morning, while everyone else was still asleep, He chose a solitary place (verse 35). Believe me, there is a time when no one else is up! You say, "But I'm not a morning person." You can become one. We're talking about success here rather than failure! Someone has said, "The difference between genius and average is what you do while everyone else is sleeping!" Get up thirty minutes before everyone else does and see what a difference it will make in your spiritual life as you spend that time memorizing God's Word.

Organize by Topic

The purpose of memorization is to be able to recall Scripture when you need it, and for the purpose you need it. *"For he mightily convinced the Jews, and that publickly, shewing by the scriptures that Jesus was Christ"* (Acts 18:28). The Bible covers hundreds of subjects and it is through these topics that it applies to our lives. (See Appendix One for a list of topics on sin and the Scriptures helping us to conquer those sins.) When Jesus was tempted by

Satan in the wilderness (Matthew 4), He did not just throw out any old verse to overcome the temptation. He used specific Old Testament Scriptures that dealt with temptation. When Satan tempted Him to turn the stones into bread to ease His hunger, He quoted Deuteronomy 8:3, "...*It is written, Man shall not live by bread alone, but by every word that proceedeth out of the mouth of God*" (Matthew 4:4).

Choose a topic. It may be an area of sin with which you are struggling like pride, worry, lust or selfishness. Get a concordance and look up that subject. You will find dozens of verses listed under the major topics of the Bible.

Get some cards and write the verses out on those "memory" cards. It doesn't matter what size you use—it depends on how good your eyes are. I used a small card about the size of a business card (a 4x6 index card cut into four equal parts). Writing the verses out on these cards is the first process of memorizing. I am aware that there are programs where you can buy the cards already printed. I had a pastor once ask me if he could "photocopy" my cards. I said, "Sure, but they'll never make it out of your desk drawer if you do." There is great value in writing the verses out in long hand. God commanded it to be done in the Old Testament.

> "*And thou shalt write them upon the posts of thy house, and on thy gates.*"—DEUTERONOMY 6:9

> "*And it shall be, when he sitteth upon the throne of his kingdom, that he shall write him a copy of this law in a book out of that which is before the priests the Levites.*"—DEUTERONOMY 17:18

> "*And thou shalt write upon them all the words of this law, when thou art passed over, that thou mayest go in unto the land which the* LORD *thy God giveth thee, a land that floweth with milk and honey; as the* LORD *God of thy fathers hath promised thee...And thou shalt write*

upon the stones all the words of this law very plainly."
—DEUTERONOMY 27:3, 8

In all of the sermon preparation, lecture notes, and writing that I have done over the years, I have never one time in my life, "cut and pasted" Scripture. Laugh if you want, but I just believe when God said to *"Study to shew thyself approved unto God..."* (2 Timothy 2:15). He wasn't thinking about "point and click," "cut and paste!" There is a disciplined process in memorization, and it starts with writing out the verses.

Now here is where my plan is a little different from others. When I decided to start memorizing seriously in 1978, I thought through how I was going to be using what I had memorized. I had two situations in my ministry when I most often needed to know the Bible—when I was preaching and when I was talking with people one-on-one in soulwinning or counseling. When I was preaching, I really didn't need to know the reference, because I could write that in my notes. I could write "Joshua 1:8." If I had memorized the verse, seeing that reference would trigger it in my mind, and I could quote it. But when I was talking with people personally, I really didn't need to know the verse, because I usually had my Bible with me and I could show them the verse (which is usually wise anyway in soulwinning), but I needed to know the reference so that I would know where to turn.

Most memory plans have cards with the reference on one side of the card and then you flip it over and the verse is written out on the reverse side. That's great, but it wasn't going to meet my need. So, I decided that I needed to memorize both the reference and the verse. I took my subject, such as "Hell" and found all of the verses in my concordance on that subject. I chose the ones I wanted to memorize and arranged them in chronological order (as they come in the Bible). This is already done in the concordance, but I chose to skip some and memorize others. I was now going to memorize that entire block of verses, in order as they come in the Bible, with both reference and the verse.

So, on the front of the card, I wrote "Hell #1" as illustrated below:

Front of the card:

Hell #1

When I flipped the card over, I wrote out the reference and the verse as illustrated:

Back of the card:

Psalm 9:17

The wicked shall be turned into hell, and all the nations that forget God.

As I memorized that subject, I memorized not only the verse but the reference with it. The first verse in that stack of cards then cued me to the second verse with its reference and text, and the second verse cued me to the third verse, etc. Thus, I memorized an entire block of verses together under one subject, all in order as they came in the Bible chronologically.

The second card in my series of verses on the subject of "Hell" looked like this:

Front of the card:

Hell #2

Back of the card:

Matthew 3:12

Whose man is in his hand, and
he will throughly purge his floor,
and gather his wheat into the
garner; but he will burn up the
chaff with unquenchable fire.

This method creates a catalog of verses in your mind under various topics, and you are able to apply them to needs at any time. If you are struggling with a particular sin, when the temptation comes, you now have a series of verses to fire at the tempter. For the soulwinner, if someone you meet says, "Well, I don't believe in a place called Hell!" immediately, you know right where to take him in the Bible and show him the evidence of God's Word. For the preacher or teacher, as you are preparing a sermon or lesson, and the text you are preaching deals with a specific subject, immediately you have your own "mental concordance" on that subject from which to draw. (Here is where all that time you thought you were wasting by "writing and memorizing verses" is going to come back and save you hours of searching for just the right verse.) If you are memorizing more than one verse in a row (for example, let's say you are on the subject of "Hell" and you want to memorize Luke 16:19–31, which is the story of the rich man and Lazarus), on the front of the card, you put "Hell # 8," or whatever number it is in your sequence. On the back you write "Luke 16:19–31." Get as many of the verses as you can on that first card and then start a second card. On the front of it you would put "Hell #8b" and continue the text on the back. If you need a third card, it would be "Hell #8c," and so on.

Now you have your stack of cards. You may have selected five or ten under a particular topic or hundreds; it all depends on how comprehensive you want to be. Just remember, you are doing this so you can use it, not just to see how many you can memorize. This isn't VBS—there are no ribbons—but this is ministry, and there are great rewards!

Let's start memorizing. We have our tool, now let's make it work!

Work Out Loud

This is why we have chosen a quiet place, alone. This is part of the process that works. You see, God emphasizes "hearing" His Word. *"But he said, Yea rather, blessed are they that hear the word of God and keep it"* (Luke 11:28). *"Therefore whosoever heareth these sayings of mine, and doeth them, I will liken him unto a wise man, which built his house upon a rock"* (Matthew 7:24). *"He that hath an ear, let him hear what the Spirit saith unto the churches"* (Revelation 3:22).

You have read it and written it out; now you are "hearing it," as phrase by phrase you commit it to memory. Some verses are easier to memorize than others so don't get frustrated. Keep going over phrases or words of the verse one at a time and then add more to it, always repeating all of it out loud. No secrets here—this takes time—but look at it as an investment. God said, *"For the merchandise of it is better than the merchandise of silver, and the gain thereof than fine gold. She is more precious than rubies: and all the things thou canst desire are not to be compared unto her"* (Proverbs 3:14–15). He adds in verse 18, *"…and happy is every one that retaineth her."*

Walk while You Memorize

Your body has rhythm. I'm sure you can tell who is coming down the hall of your house by their walk. Little children are able to memorize the words to songs long before they can read because the words are written to the rhythm of music. I can guarantee that you will memorize Scripture faster by walking than sitting in a chair (or behind the wheel of your car stuck in rush hour traffic).

I was preaching at a teen camp one summer. I came out of my room and there was a young girl about fifteen sitting on a rock with her Bible in her lap and she was crying. I went over to her and asked her why she was crying. She said, "I've been trying to memorize this verse for the last thirty minutes and I just can't get it!" (She was trying to earn points for her team.) I took her Bible from her asking which verse it was that she was struggling with? I said, "Let me hear what you've got so far." Quite honestly, she didn't have much. She stammered through the first couple of words and got stuck. I must admit it was a rather difficult verse. I said, "Stand up." I pointed to a trailer about fifty yards down the sidewalk from where we were standing. "Take the Bible and walk toward that trailer and come back. Do exactly what you have been trying to do to memorize the verse while you walk. I'll wait for you right here and when you get back, we'll see how much you know." She looked at me like I was weird, but took off. She made it to the trailer and turned around. (I could see her lips moving as she was mouthing the words.) She got about ten feet from the trailer and began running toward me, yelling, "I've got it! I've got it!" Sure enough, she did too. Now granted, she had been working on it before my experiment, but the rhythm of her walk sealed it in her mind.

Try it—the exercise won't hurt you either. I have been in small guest quarters at times and had only enough space to take three or four steps and turn around and walk back, but it makes all the difference in the world. The rhythm in your body will make the verse not only a part of your mind but also a part of your entire being. And you will sense the power of God's Word as you use it in your life.

Review, Review, Review

Repetition is the key to learning. Some memory plans will tell you that if you say the verse a certain number of times for a certain number of days, you'll never forget it. That doesn't seem to work for me. I have to keep reviewing every verse. I have often stated, "We've all had more than one telephone number in our lives, but we probably only remember the one we are using now." Use it or lose it, as they say. Until you have learned your entire stack of verses under a subject, you'll need to go through all of them every day. Once you have that whole topic memorized, you may be able to reduce your review of that subject to once a week. Perhaps later, less, but you'll have to keep going over them.

I figured it out one day. For every verse I have memorized over these years, counting all of the time it took to write out the verse, the memorization time and the review time, I have spent two hundred hours on every verse that I have memorized! Now do you still think I have a photographic memory? I mean, really—I could teach a bad parrot to quote a verse in two hundred hours! Don't tell me you just can't memorize or you're too old or whatever. You can, but like I said, it's "time and work."

Set Goals of Time

Once you start memorizing and using God's Word, you'll not be able to get verses written on cards fast enough. Let me caution you. Don't set a goal of how many verses you want to memorize in a day, week, month or year. The truth is some passages are much easier to memorize than others. You are already familiar with them, or they are narrative or story-type in nature and thus the material flows very easily and logically. Others are not like that. The biblical wording is sometimes different than the way we might say it today, and the sentence might be compounded in nature. You might spend several days on one verse. You will get discouraged if you set your goals on the number of verses. Set a goal of the amount of "time" you are going to spend daily, weekly, monthly, on memorization. Commit yourself to that time no matter what; and as you do, the number of verses will add up over the months and years.

In conclusion, let me say that some of the most enjoyable times of my life have been spent alone memorizing God's Word. In the wee hours of the morning, it's just God and me with His Word. Some might call it a sacrifice, but God went to a lot of trouble to give us His Word, and my effort to put it into my life seems pretty small in comparison. I have found that He has blessed that effort over these years.

Oh, how I have enjoyed seeing God use the Scripture that I have hidden in my heart. It has helped me in those moments of temptation, and I have had the joy of sharing it with countless others through preaching, teaching, counseling and soulwinning. In Haggai 2:19A, God asks a question, *"Is the seed yet in the barn?"* In Luke 8:11, Jesus declared, *"The seed is the word of God."* Every spring my Dad would buy seed corn. That seed never produced a harvest while in the bag stacked in the barn. We had to get it out into the field. That required lots of time and effort, but once done there was a great harvest. The seed of God's Word doesn't accomplish anything if left in the barn of a Book. But if you will take the time and effort to sow it in your heart, you will enjoy a wonderful harvest.

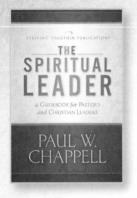

Visit us online

strivingtogether.com

dailyintheword.org

wcbc.edu

lancasterbaptist.org

paulchappell.com